PATHWAY TO
Greatness

JOHNNY MARTINEZ-CARROLL

To Bob,
thanks for supporting me
today!

[signature]

ISBN 979-8-88540-483-9 (paperback)
ISBN 979-8-88616-980-5 (digital)

Christian Faith Publishing
832 Park Avenue
Meadville, PA 16335
www.christianfaithpublishing.com

Printed in the United States of America

This book is dedicated to my mother, Sanie Martinez, and my dad, Mason Carroll. I live and breathe because of you. You gave me life. I can only hope and pray that you are both proud of me and the work that I do, whether it's writing books or helping people like you taught me.

Thank you, Sue, for supporting me and putting up with me, long hours in my home office writing or at the dining room table with my laptop for long hours at a time. I would like to thank my children who also inspire me to be even greater in life! Thank you so much for believing in your dad! I said that I would mention Thor, my dog. Thor, thank you for being patient with Daddy when you wanted to play and I was busy writing!

I have my family, friends and so many readers that have thanked me and shared with me how my first book inspired them. This book is dedicated to you as well. Your love and support is truly appreciated.

Snook, Texas! I never left far from home. Snook will always be home to me. I love the fact that I know the people and the same people I see daily support the kid who never strayed far from his roots. Thanks again, Snook, Texas!

Thank you to my sisters, whom I love with all my heart, Margaret, Mary, Crystal, Carolyn, Harriet, Sharon, and Ulanda.

Thank you to my work team at Methodist Children's Home and to the wonderful families we serve. I dedicate this book to you as well. You were made for greatness! Since my first book, *The Silent Dreamer*, I have met so many wonderful people in person and on social media. Thank you for the amazing connections! God bless each one of you!

Introduction

This book was written as a follow up to my first book, *The Silent Dreamer*. My hope and goal for this book is to let others know that we are all destined for greatness! I love to just use and say the word, *greatness*! I can feel something special about understanding that we are made in the very image of God. We were created for greatness! In this book, I want to discuss areas of growth in order to become the great person God intended for us to become in this life. I also wanted to share more stories of my upbringing, being raised in poverty on a farm where cotton was king in the early sixties. In my first book, I introduced you to the kid who grew up poor, dropped out of high school, and later received his college degree. That same kid grew up with dreams of doing great things in life. The journey has been both a rough and smooth ride, mostly rough! This book is intended to help you discover principles in helping you to become greater as a person and in life in general. You and I were made to be the best that God made us to be! I cannot even begin to write without mentioning people who have influenced me along my journey. Most have passed on and now live in heaven. That great cloud of witnesses in my personal life, still influence me today! I truly believe we were put on this earth to inspire and influence others. The last few years I have made it my goal in life to influence others to live the best life possible. I have received so many compliments about my first book, *The Silent Dreamer*. I have heard from people from all walks in life telling me how much my book inspired them to share their story. A few were even inspired to write a book, my daughter included. Hard work and supportive people in your circle are still the best way to succeed in life today. I have had the honor and pleasure of having both in my life. *Pathway to Greatness* is to inspire you to continue to dream and dream big! This book was written during the pandemic, which changed so much our everyday life. In some ways, it brought us closer together, and in some ways, it divided us too. Mask or no mask, shot or no shot! But I think we can all agree that it made us look at life and appreciate the precious time that we so much take for granted. It made me think each day that my time is special and so are the people around me each day. I had my share of losing loved ones during this pandemic as well: friends and family members. I wrote this book thinking each day my life is precious and I want to do so much in my personal and professional life. So much work is left for me to do! I will be the first to say that I get discouraged and disappointed. I have bad days just like anyone else, but my mindset is always to remember why I am here and to never forget that our lives were made for greatness!

Becoming Greater!

I do not know about you, but I am always looking at where I can improve in both my personal and professional life, looking at ways to improve how I react toward trials and challenges, how I respond to things that go on around me. Ask yourself this question, What is holding me back? What is keeping me from moving forward? If you are like me, it is the person in the mirror. I can look at myself and answer both of those questions. It is always *me*! As a kid growing up, I really did not have a support system that backed me up. I had a loving mom and dad, but they both were not incredibly supportive of me. They were busy just making ends meet, providing for our family. No one ever said to me, "You were made for greatness." To be honest, even as an adult, I never really heard those words from anyone in my small circle.

As a young parent, I would tell my kids that they could achieve anything they set out to do, that they could accomplish things if they applied hard work and discipline. I know that sounds like something we have heard all of our lives: hard work pays off, seek for the sky, the sky is the limit. I know that as a young parent, I wanted my kids to achieve the things that I never got to accomplish, mainly a college degree.

Let us look at the word *greatness*! Being larger than ordinary. You were made to be larger in terms of a state of being. You were made to be greater than normal. You achieve this by creating vision, practicing positive habits, developing a champions mindset, turning adversity into advantages. Yes, you were meant for all these things. Being great has nothing to do with being better than anyone, let us get that clear. It has all to do with being the best you that you can be!

Let us take a closer look at being great. It requires creating vision, as we said earlier. I recall as a kid, I did look at where I was, growing up in extreme poverty and literally dreaming of how I would ever get out of poverty and living in those conditions. I can honestly say that back then I certainly did not feel like I was made to be great! Neither did I feel like anything great would come from living under those conditions: no running water or indoor plumbing. Nothing was great about that at all. I can say that my vision was to eventually make my life better through hard work and determination. Before we go any further, let us just say that your past does not define your future. Nothing stays the same; everything eventually changes! Remember that person in the mirror? Eventually that person changes too! Greatness can also be defined by being the real you, being true to yourself, being who you were meant to be, discovering your gift.

As I write this, I can see that this is a lot to take in, but let us just take it step by step as we continue this journey of greatness. I was born and raised on a cotton plantation. We were extremely poor. We had very little in terms of material things. Did I mention that we were extremely poor? I genuinely believe that humble beginnings define us. They follow us throughout life. I will never forget how I grew up and where I grew up. I know that those times made an impact on me. I grew up an incredibly quiet kid. It wasn't until a few years ago that I discovered my personality had a name: I am an introvert. I did some research on why introverts are the way they are and how they function in this world that seems to have so many people that are dying to talk and give their opinions! I also found out that I am in the company of greatness when it comes to famous introverts, such as Mother Theresa and Rosa Parks, just to name a few. When I see the contributions that these two women made in our society, I am in awe. They have always been two of my favorite heroes. I have studied both and have for some time held them both in high regards. Greatness come in all sizes, as these two great women were both small in stature. In the Bible, the psalms writer mentions that we are "fearfully and wonderfully made in the image of God." That verse is found in Psalms 139. In my previous book, *The Silent Dreamer*, I mentioned my parents many times throughout the book.

In my eyes, they were both great people with different but yet similar personalities. Both were quiet by nature, and both would give you anything they had to give if you needed something. For instance, my dad had vision. He saw the greater picture if you will. He would prepare in advance. He looked past the present moment.

Let us look back to what we said earlier about having vision and becoming great. This also means that you see greatness in others! You also bring out that quality in other people, those who are around you: your family, friends, team at work, at church. Think about it, greatness is all around you. People are doing amazing things every day, and most are not even being recognized. They are simply being themselves, being real. I see it every day with my team at work, teammates who are going above and beyond to make life better for the people in the community that they work and live in.

When you look into the mirror, what do you see? This question will get the response of many different answers. For me personally, I see someone who is still not as brave as I would want to be. I still struggle with speaking my mind at times, and to be honest, there are times that I would love to just give some people a piece of my mind! But for those who know me, they know that is not who I am. Being great does take bravery, and I can say that this is an area that I continue to work and make progress. Looking in the mirror, I do see where I want to be in life. I do see that I have some obstacles that have not been conquered yet. My vision is focused on my impact on those who are around me each day: my family, friends, and teammates at work. My vision includes my circle of clients that I serve daily. I want them to be great as well.

Developing Positive Habits

I have heard that it takes twenty-one days to drop a bad habit. I think of this each time I try to kick my soda-drinking habit! My weakness is Dr. Pepper and chips! Developing good habits can be challenging, but like all things that you want that are good for you, it takes discipline. If becoming a greater version of ourselves requires developing positive habits, where do we start? We start one day at a time! One habit at a time. I just thought, as I write this, that it is the third day of a new year and I still have not had a soda to drink! I know it has only been three days, but that is a small victory for me. I will take it! The year 2020 was a year where we lived and worked through a pandemic. Now in early 2021, we still are living in times of uncertainty, but we remain hopeful in the new year. We have had to change how we normally do things with social distancing and wearing of mask out in public. We have had to develop habits that continue in our daily life just to live during this awful pandemic, but for me personally, I have developed the habit of reading more, especially things that are positive and motivating. I love a good book or article that makes me think and want to be better as a person.

During this pandemic, I have learned to look out for others more, being of help to those who need it if at all possible. Social distancing has put a damper on what we would normally do for others, not so much available during a pandemic. For instance, I have delivered food boxes to people, only to leave them at their doorsteps. Developing the habit of helping others is something that I was taught as a child by watching my parents help others. I honestly believe that the quality of becoming a great person is developed in what we do for others in time of need. I have had the honor of knowing and working with people who make it a habit of helping others and making life better for them, providing food and basic necessities. Get in the habit of motivating others to do the best they can do. Be a cheerleader to those around you. I recall working for a local nonprofit with a team of about twelve team members. Although I was not the leader or supervisor, I took it upon myself to motivate those around me with a daily email of inspiration. I learned that you do not have to be the leader to be the leader! The title is just that, a title. Greatness involves leading even when it is not your job or you do not have the title to do so. I have also been the unofficial leader in many places that I have worked at. Being the positive one is what I want to be known for. This should be your goal as well.

I have also learned that not every leader is made to lead. I have worked at places where the leadership was great and places where it was not so great. Greatness starts at the top. The effects trickle down. The same applies with the lack of leadership. Not sure why some bosses do not get this concept and wonder why work morale is so low! Remember that mirror we talked about earlier? Maybe they should look into that mirror. Developing positive habits take time. They do not happen overnight, but the results can last a lifetime. The scripture says that iron sharpens iron. In order to develop positive habits, the company that you keep may need to change. You might just have to associate yourself with positive people. Find people who look to lift up people and not those who tear them down. You were not only made to be great, but you were made to inspire and motivate those around you! I know that looks like a lot of responsibility, but you were made for it! I believe in you! I truly mean that. I have often thought many times of where I would be in life if only someone had told me at an early age, "I believe in you" and "You were made for greatness." Words spoken to us as positive affirmation can make us, and the lack of it can break us! Words can either help or hurt us. I can remember things that were said to me years ago that to this very day still hurt. The sting is still there.

Developing positive habits takes time and practice as much as it takes discipline. You must put into practice what you want to learn, what you want to change about yourself. Trust me I speak from experience here. My mind is filled with what I need to do, but whether I am willing to do those things is another story! With persistence and determination, you can do the impossible, the unthinkable. You can achieve whatever you set out to do. Take it from a high school dropout to college graduate. Take it from someone who was destined to be "nothing," living in poverty. When your support system is limited, this will limit you as well. It's not easy being positive, but when you want better, you seek better. At some point and time, the light comes on. It becomes a new day! I love this quote that I saw on Facebook once. It read, "If you hang around me long enough, I will brainwash you into believing you can do anything you set out to do." This is true about me, and it should be true about you as well! We are living in times of so many uncertainties. We need all the encouraging, uplifting of one another that we can get. We need to always be ready to make someone's day, be someone's sunshine, their reason to smile!

Mindset of a Champion

Thoughts become things! This statement is so true. What we think we bring about it! The mind will wander wherever you take it. What is it to think like a champion? And whoever said that champions think different from any other person? But in my opinion, they do think differently. Any champion that I know, whether it's on the sports field, boardroom, speaker, author, etc., they think and feel that they are the best at what they do. They have a "can do" mentality. They let nothing stop them from being the very best. Champions train and take care of themselves like no other. They work their tails off! I recall when I had my first book, *The Silent Dreamer*, published. I remember talking to a friend who was also a published author, and I followed her on Twitter. She had also did a Ted Talk, so she was very established. I remember our conversation; and what I said to her was that, after publishing my first book, I felt so much confidence, felt like I could achieve anything that I set out to do. I felt like a champion! Not only did I feel like one, but my thinking was also like a champion! Maybe for the first time in my adult life, I felt worthy. I felt like somebody. Let's look back a little here. Let's go to my childhood, that shy little kid who would jump if you said boo to him! That kid was far from being champion status. Growing up, my dad would be the only person that I would say had champion thinking. Nothing rattled him. He was tough under pressure. I could go on and on about him. I will say this about myself, growing up in poverty does make you tough minded. You learn to make do with what you have. It's a lesson you learn to live with, the mindset of a champion!

The ability to move from failure to failure with no loss of enthusiasm makes you a champion. (Winston Churchill)

I get so much from this amazing quote. I see fight regardless of failure. I see resilience too. I see that no matter what happens here, even in failure, my mindset is still on winning! I am a champion despite my current situation. *I am not defeated!* I personally know people with this mentality. I am sure you do as well. People with "never quit" in them. They will find the good in all things, the grass is always green, the skies are always blue, even when the sun is not shining! What can I learn from this season? I love that kind of personality in people. This is what greatness looks like. It doesn't mean that all is going well in their world, but it does mean that the current situation does not define how they react to it. Greatness has a way of pressing forward, moving past obstacles. No limits or boundaries will hold you back. I say to you, this is a great time to mention, you were made for greatness! You have vision. You think like a champion. Let's move on to the next phase: turning adversities into advantages.

Turning Adversity to Advantages

This part of greatness I can fully relate with, I like to call it taking closed doors and turning them to open opportunities. I know all about closed doors, missed opportunities, so on and so forth. Did I mention that greatness requires thick skin? It means that even amid having your dream swept away from you, being told you are not smart enough for a position, you had your heart set on. You still have to keep a level head and a straight face. Remember I grew up in the cotton fields. Summers were hot; the cotton rows were long. I did not see then that it was all part of the process: hot summer heat, working long hours in the field. I am sure people had written me off. He will never be anything in life! I am sure if you are reading this right now that people said the same thing about you as well. He or she is destined for nothing in life, but here you are today. You are greater than that! You are more than your greatest adversity; you are more than a conqueror.

Greatness brings adversity with it so many times. The struggle is real as they say. We don't always see rejection and adversity that comes with it or closed doors along the way that serve as obstacles in the process of trying to make progress. I recently had a family member tell me that she enjoyed my previous book, *The Silent Dreamer*. She mentioned to me how much she learned about me that she never knew. She shared with me how she was inspired to return back to school to finish her degree. I told her to go for it. I also told her that it's not meant to be easy, but it can be done. People are doing this every day. Nothing is impossible with hard work and a great support system. It helps also to have God in your corner! To be honest, that alone will sustain you on your journey to accomplishments.

Nothing worth having in life comes easy. We have all heard that all our lives. You got to put in the work. If it were easy, everyone would be doing it! It takes commitment and discipline like crazy. You put all that you have into your goals and dreams. You cry some while you pray even more. I remember this story of my first job that wasn't working in the cotton fields. I was in high school, and I worked as a dishwasher at a local college campus. Remember the phrase, "He only had one job to do"? Well, that was me. All I had to do was sort out silverware, but because of my shyness and not asking questions, I let the silverware pile up! I mean, it was so piled up, and we were so behind because of my neglecting to check it. We then had to work almost till midnight catching up and sorting out silverware. That night, while at the time clock punching out, I thought, *Will I come back tomorrow? Will I quit this job on my first day!* My supervisor, Daniel, told me that it was okay, that tomorrow will be a better day. Those words spoken to me put confidence in me, and I returned the next day, and it was a better day! Words of encouragement spoken in times of adversity carry so much power and make such a great impact to the person receiving them. Setbacks set us up for comebacks. For me, it's been the fear of failure so many times in my life as an adult. Most people have this same fear, so when a little adversity comes, they run and hide. They talk themselves out of starting anything. I can certainly relate. It wasn't until a few years ago that I got my bravery. Better late than never, right? I have learned that if I want it, go get it! Adversity doesn't always mean no, maybe a delay. It might involve a detour of some sort, but it does not certainly have to mean *no*!

You were made for greatness in a world filled with so much hatred and with so many people who will do their best to stop your progress. Like the saying goes, not everyone will clap for you when you win! I recall years ago when I was enrolled in college, working full time and working at making myself better, wanting to achieve an educational goal in life that I should have done years ago but did not for whatever the reason. I was working, and I had some coworkers tell me, "Why are you doing that now? Aren't you too old to be in school? What would a college degree do for you this late in life?" I could have easily just quit, could have listened to the negativity and just given up on my goals, but I didn't. That fueled me to continue. I was working to better myself, not them. Your goals should be for you as well. You are doing things to better yourself, and in doing so, people around you will feel your impact. They will become better. You will be the example to inspire and motivate them. That's how greatness works through adversity!

There are times when you have to walk alone through adversity. To be honest, most of the time you do walk alone. It's not an easy road to travel, but you walk in faith. You believe in the outcome. You have faith in the process. You walk with the one who got you to this point. Yes, remember earlier we talked about having God on our side. He is with you every step of the way. Remember the classic poem "Footprints in the Sand," the one set of prints. That was when he carried you! Friends, after reading this first chapter, prepare yourself for greatness! Go out and be great today. Be the best you that you can possibly be. You have some tools to work with. You have vision, you have the mind of a champion, and you can turn adversity into advantages! And for a bonus, you can add this one also: you were made in the living image of God! And he had plans for you even before you were ever born! You were destined for greatness. You were made for this moment of greatness in your life. Your greatness moment is right now! I want to share with you traits of greatness in this book. I want to look at areas in our lives where we can adjust to a life of greatness. We already have what it takes within us! As a young kid growing up in those cotton fields, I had it within me back then also! Greatness is within you as well! You have all you need to be great. Let's take it a step further to greatness!

Life lesson from this chapter:

I was created for greatness. I have greatness within me! From this day forward, I will be *great*!

> **"For I know the plans I have for you," declares the Lord. "Plans to prosper you and not harm you, plans to give you hope and a future."**
>
> **—Jeremiah 29:11(KJV)**

Becoming Grateful!

It all starts and ends with a grateful heart! What are you grateful for today? If you're like me, you are grateful for many things! I have mentioned so many times of my childhood growing up in extreme poverty, having so little but being thankful for all we had. We take so much for granted. I take so much for granted. I have failed many times to just be thankful for even the small things I have been blessed with. Becoming the best that we can be starts with being thankful for everything we have. Let's look at some key points of being grateful. I believe that you must be humble. Humility is key to becoming a better version of yourself. Gratitude is a valuable lesson in life. We have so many things to be grateful for.

If we learned anything about the year 2020 it was that life is precious. Life during a pandemic has taught us so much. We are grateful for family, our jobs. We are thankful for life itself! So many people lost loved ones because of this pandemic. So many lost their jobs and businesses. People were evicted from their homes. It has been so depressing to watch the news daily and see the stories of people hurting. Being thankful is something we have learned to express as often as possible. This would be a great time to just say, "Thank you, Lord, for everything!"

Years ago, I worked maintenance making electrical repairs at the county jail. I remember working in a cell and an inmate had posted on the wall this quote: "Lord, I don't need more to be grateful. I just need to be more grateful." Let that sink in for a minute. I never forgot these profound words. I also realized that inspiration could come from anywhere, even a jail cell. I learned that here was a person who was locked up and here was someone who was also thankful. I know that I have mentioned so many times about my childhood, growing up with so little. God bless my poor mother who took nothing for granted and made everything we had last as long as it could. I never really knew that we were poor. Everyone around us had either the same as we did or less. I can honestly say that being grateful has made me more sensitive to the needs of others. I believe that having a spirit of gratitude does that to a person, what an awesome trait to becoming a better you!

**God has never stopped being good.
We've just stop being grateful.**

Here is something you can try: pay it forward. Do something nice for a total stranger. This act does not have to be a big act of kindness; it could be as simple as paying for a cup of coffee. I love seeing others being blessed by total strangers. These stories bring me joy. Nothing can top that feeling than being the one who is doing the blessings! Again, I ask you, What are you thankful for? Gratitude is something that I taught my kids growing up, and as a child myself, my parents taught me to be thankful and to be respectful also. When was the last time that you were thankful for dirty dishes? Dirty dishes means that you had food on those plates! Growing up, a skillet of potatoes was something to be thankful for. A pot of beans was a blessing, and we said thank you! What we often complain about, someone else would be thankful for. When we look at our troubles, we must remember that someone would be glad to trade problems with us in a minute. As the saying goes, nothing last forever, including our troubles. Each day is a gift from God to find something to be thankful for: the sun, wind, rain, green grass, the air that we breathe.

When I sit and think and look around me, I see so much that I simply take for granted. I'm sure you do as well. But having a spirit of gratitude puts us in touch with the goodness of God. We witness firsthand how he supplies all of our needs. Years ago, I was out of work for almost two years. I got laid off from my job as an electrician. Times were hard raising a family with no job, but I never had a bill go unpaid, and we always had food to eat, God always provided! *Always!*

Gratitude requires patience. We don't always like waiting for things to happen, but we must learn to wait. I believe that good things come to those who wait and those who wait with a thankful spirit. People who wait patiently and pray for change or something good to happen in their favor will eventually receive it.

As I mentioned earlier in this chapter about me being out of work for almost two years, I looked for work at many places during that time, interviews that did not go anywhere. But finally, one day, I got the call that I was hired. The job would be in a field that would be new to me. Nothing to do with electricity as I was used to. I was a direct-care assistant. I worked at a mental health-care facility, a life-changing experience, to say the least, but it was a job that I grew to love, and yes, I was very thankful. I remember my niece who was young at the time, maybe ten or twelve, saying to me, "Uncle Johnny, I was praying for you." I never forgot those words, and always give thanks for the prayers of others. If we are going to become better at being ourselves, we must always be thankful for the people who mention us by name in prayer. I am so thankful for the people in my life who I can call or text and say to them, "Will you pray for me?" I don't have to give specifics that's all they need to know, and they will pray for me. That is the type of person that I want to be also, and I have friends who ask me to do the same for them. I am thankful for every opportunity to mention someone's name in prayer. God knows I know many people have prayed for me in my lifetime. Prayer warriors, we call them. Be thankful for those who are praying for you.

One of my goals each year is to be more grateful, to be more thankful than the year before, but we should be more thankful each day, more than the day before! We have so much to be grateful for each day, like mentioned earlier, especially during this pandemic. So many lost lives even while I write this book. We are learning and experiencing daily the importance of life itself, how fragile life is. If we are to become better at who we are, we must fully grasp the concept of gratitude. We must take time during the day to take inventory for all that is good in our life and say thank you!

Gratitude helps you fall in love with the life you
already have. (Unknown)

Every day brings so much to be grateful for. We must learn to
look around us and just be thankful for all the provisions we have
in our lives. We must share our blessings with those who are around
us. This is vital in our journey of becoming greater each day we live.
I can look around me as I write and think of so much that I am so
grateful for. I am so blessed to have the necessities of life: a home,
reliable transportation, my job and career, and, of course, the obvious, my family and friends. Life is filled with so many blessings. Your
life is filled with blessings as well. Let's look around us, and let's agree
that we are living a blessed life right now. Our health and strength is
a blessing we should never take for granted. I grew up with very little
in terms of material things, but we had what we needed to get by, or
least in my eyes, I thought we did: food, a roof over our head, clothes
to wear—the basic things that most kids today take for granted.

We should spend every moment teaching our youth of today
the importance of being grateful and thankful. I have heard, and you
may have heard this as well, that we are living among an ungrateful
generation. I believe there is some truth to that. Our generation today
takes so much for granted, but then don't we all at times? I need to be
more grateful at times myself. If I am to become better, I need to be
more thankful each day for all the blessings around me. I am guilty
of this so many times over and over again. I recently volunteered
with a local nonprofit that makes bunk beds for children who do not
have a bed to sleep on. I really felt good and honored to help with
this project. We take for granted the bed that we sleep in each night,
something that we really do not think about, but unfortunately, not
everyone has this luxury. Again, this is another thing to be thankful
for in our daily lives: to be able to sleep in a warm, comfortable bed.

Even as I write this, I can think of so many things that I am
thankful for today that I just took for granted. This certainly an area
that I want to improve on my way to become better and greater in my
everyday walk. This would be a good time to stop and think about
all the things we are thankful for that we often take for granted. Stop

and close your eyes for a minute. Look at what you have that is there every day but you just do not really think much about them. I take so much for granted, not realizing that blessing are right in front of me all the time. There is so much to be thankful for.

I see hurting people each day with my job. I consider it an honor to be in position to help hurting people each day, people who would trade problems with me in a heartbeat. I serve people who are thankful for whatever they can get in some circumstances. They just need the help at that given time. Becoming greater and better requires a thankful and grateful spirit. This is deeper than saying a prayer before we eat our meals. This is much deeper than that. This is recognizing in our hearts that we are so blessed with so much more than we can see, that even in our troubles we can still be grateful. Let's be honest, our lives could change in a split second. Life is full of surprises, some pleasant and some not so pleasant. Things can change unexpectedly—the loss of a job, a bad doctor report, death of a loved one. So many other things can happen, but can we remain thankful and grateful in those dark times?

Happiness is not having what you want. It is appreciating what you have. (Unknown)

I can look back on my early life as a new dad with a young child and newly married. Times were simpler then. Looking back, we only had the basics to get by: food, clothes, and shelter. We were living from paycheck to paycheck but thinking all along that I was blessed, even when I was short on money many times, okay, pretty much all the time! But God was good. He provided and still does! Learn to be thankful and grateful for his provisions. He promises to provide. Trust at those promises. Thank him for his promises. Just while writing this book, so much has changed in my life, so much to be grateful for. I am thankful for just simple peace of mind while living in this new year of uncertainty. The pandemic continues, and yet my vision is clear. I am thankful for that.

My life has taken so many twists and turns. The kid from the cotton fields; the kid wearing hand-me-down clothes; eating beans, rice, and potatoes almost daily—that kid has so much to be thankful for. The kid who grew up and as a man has had so many doors closed to his face. That man is thankful today. Yes, closed doors are to be thankful for too! Those doors lead to open ones! I am where I am today because of closed door and missed opportunities. I remain thankful. I am thankful for my family, friends, my job and career, my relationships, my health, my mind and heart that wants to serve others, so many things and people in my life at this very moment. I am so thankful for having a loving mother who raised me to be grateful and to love others. May she rest in peace forever! She did her very best to provide for her children with the little that she had. Job well done, Momma. You earned your rest! I literally watched my mother die, one ailment after another. I never heard her complain once, a soldier till the end.

Gratitude is truly everything. What are you grateful for today at this very moment? I am truly thankful and grateful for the opportunities that have been set before me since the release of my first book. Whether it's appearing for a book event or being invited to talk about my book, *The Silent Dreamer*, I am always thankful for the opportunity. I love the platform it has put me on, to be able to share with others the good news that life has its obstacles but that you can overcome anything set against you. If you put in the hard work and you surround yourself with people who love and support you, the possibilities are endless. Yes, I am learning each day to have a thankful and grateful spirit. This is truly the only way to live in this life and to be successful at the same time. A grateful attitude will take you far in life. It is so important to be thankful for all of life's blessings, both large and small. Blessings are all around us. I am seeing this more and more as I grow older. I am so blessed, and I am seeing more blessings poured out over my family and friends all the time. Yes, becoming greater requires becoming more thankful and grateful. I remember once reading somewhere this quote: "If we engulf ourselves in serving others, our problems in life will go away." That makes sense to me; I totally get it. I know from personal experience, when I spend time helping others through volunteering, my mind is taken away from the problems going on in my life. My complete focus is helping others. For that, I am truly grateful, not that they have problems, but that I am able to help someone else while they are going through something. Becoming more thankful is key to becoming greater! I am realizing more each day that the more thankful that I am, the more I see opportunities around me. I find myself asking God to help me to see the small things that I take for granted so many times.

What are some small things that you are grateful in your life today? What about a kind word spoken to you by a friend or coworker? A compliment about your work ethic or kindness that you have shown to someone? Maybe it's the opportunity to do something for a total stranger? These and many other examples are small things to be thankful for in our lives. Things are opportunities to be even greater and to make a huge impact on someone else's life. Becoming greater involves developing an attitude of gratitude. We are going to see this a lot in this book: being more grateful. My life is truly a blessed life. I am sure that your life is just as blessed.

I recently had lunch with a friend. I shared with her how my life has changed since having my first book published. I shared with her about the wonderful people I have had the pleasure of meeting, the connections behind my book, *The Silent Dreamer*. I am so thankful for the platform it has put me on. Not famous, nor rich, just thankful for the people I get to share my story with. Just for the opportunity to share with others about my life's journey, the road traveled and the obstacles that were in my way. I am very thankful, so appreciative for each opportunity I have to share with others the message that you were made to be great!

Life lesson from this chapter:

If I am going to be greater in life, I must learn to be more thankful and grateful for the blessings around me! Blessings both big and small!

Becoming Kinder!

Sounds simple doesn't it. Truth is, becoming a better version of yourself requires being kind. The world needs so much of this today. Think of what a world we would have to live in if everyone were just kind to each other. The current state of our nation seems to be in turmoil. We have so much hatred in the news. Social media is filled with stories after stories of people being mean to one another. It's sickening, to be honest. One of the greatest lessons that we can teach our children is to simply be nice, to be kind toward one another. At an early age, we teach our young ones to be nice, play fair, take turns, and share your toys! People need to know that you care for them; they need to know that someone gives a damn about them. I have heard some say that people are meaner today than years ago. What do you think? I know this one thing: people in my day helped each other more. Just my opinion. People are doing great acts of kindness every day all over the world. Make sure you are one for them. Remember the golden rule: treat others like you would want to be treated. We were taught this rule at home as a kid and then again in Sunday school class. Simply to be kind to others. Showing kindness reflects a quality in you that says you have empathy for people, that you care for more than just yourself, you put yourself in their situation. I just don't get how some people can be so mean. Is it safe to say that maybe they are that way because they don't love themselves? And if they have no love for themselves, how can they feel love for anyone else and be kind to them? I think it's safe to say that showing kindness requires love! Love for yourself and love for those around you that it makes you want to be kind to them. It comes naturally. But in a world where there is so much hatred and people being mean toward one another, where do we start? I think by now you have figured out that it begins with you! It begins with you and me. Yes, we must each do our part in showing kindness in this unkind world. "Make America kind again" is a hashtag that I used when posting stories or pictures on Facebook.

To make a difference in someone's life, you don't have to be brilliant, rich, beautiful, or perfect. You just have to care. (Mandy Hale)

I have had the opportunity or the honor of being around so many people who are also the kindest people on the planet. People who give their all in making life better for the less fortunate. Showing kindness gives us the opportunity to be an example to our youth. They are watching. Growing up, my dad set the best example for me. I saw him countless times show kindness to others. I got a chance to see many times his spirit of compassion toward others, life lessons that I never forgot.

In my lifetime, I have been on both ends of kindness, the giver and receiver; and I must admit, both sides feel good! I have had people show me kindness, and I was not expecting it at all. The Bible talks about the favor of God. The favor of God simply put means the power that changes things for us. Let's look at this closer. Someone does a simple act of kindness for you. You sense it as favor from God, and your life is completely different. I recently saw a story of a group of people coming together to show kindness. They totally remodeled the house of an elderly person who had needed repairs but no funds to have them done. This act of kindness and others are being done every day. Some are extreme like the remodeling of a home; some are simple like the paying of a bill. Whether big or small, I believe it takes an act of God to move on the hearts of His people to do such things. Compassion, kindness, empathy—these are all qualities to becoming a better you! Kindness is contagious. Years ago, when I was over a group of people at a church I was attending, we would go out in the community and do a project together. We would go out and help work on a Habitat for Humanity house or visit the local nursing home and visit with residents who lived there. The number in the group varied, but we had people who were eager to go and help. One person doing an act of kindness is all it takes to spark a movement. Before you know it, you have a chain reaction of people doing great things! All it takes is for you to start it. What will you do today to get something kind happening in your community, at work perhaps? It really does not matter where you show up with kindness in your heart. It could be at the checkout line at the store, anywhere. Kindness is needed all over the place! The world needs kind people like you. The world needs a big dose of kindness.

What I have learned the most about living through the pandemic of 2020 and into 2021, people are hurting and people are coming together to help in communities. I have seen local churches step up and provide food as some food pantries are running low. I have had the pleasure of volunteering at a local church food distribution during this pandemic. I was able to see firsthand kindness at work. Every Friday people would drive by the church parking lot and get fresh fruits and vegetables, milk and bread items. I saw the same people each week. You got to know them by name. Both the volunteers and the people receiving the food—it was a beautiful thing to witness. Kindness is about good things happening to deserving people. If you just read that last statement, you are probably agreeing! People who are good and deserve good in return, you might say. How about thinking of this? Kindness is meant for all people. When you master this concept, you will be on your way of becoming a better person. You will be on your way to becoming greater!

Being Kind to Unkind People

I grew up watching the kindest person on the planet help people, that person was my dad. I saw him do things regularly for people I probably wouldn't lift a finger to help! You probably know some people like that as well. It's easy to do something good for someone we know, or better yet, someone we like. Jesus taught us to love our enemies. He also taught us about doing good to those who hate us and for us to pray for them and for those who use and mistreat you. This verse is found in the book of Matthew 5:44. My father never quoted Bible verses to me. He just showed me how to be by his actions. As a young child, I always knew my dad was a good person with a huge heart for helping people. To be honest, I never knew him to say a harsh word toward anyone and nothing negative about any person, ever! A quiet man, I can relate to that. His actions spoke for him time and time again. You and I have been and will continue to be in the position where we will rise and help people that we might find undeserving of our help. All of God's children are worthy. They are all precious in His sight. We all are. Where would we be if it were not for His grace? One thing to always consider, people are fighting battles that we have no knowledge of all over the world. You never know what a person is going through, so be nice always! I mentioned earlier about the church group that I led years ago. It was called RAKE (Random Acts of Kindness Everywhere). I learned so much being involved with this amazing group of people. I have learned when you help people, you don't care about their political affiliation. You don't even care if they are Christians or not, saved or unsaved. None of those things matter. What matters is what can I do for you to help you be in a better situation. We are all made in the image of God. I must remind myself of that many times when working with people. It does not matter what kind of opinion I may have of them; we are all his children. When we become kind people, we become the hands and feet of Jesus. We were put here on this earth to do the very thing we may ask at times, "What would Jesus do?" Remember the phase back in the nineties, WWJD? We are here to do his will; and if his will means to help the poor, the elderly, the widow and the orphan, then that's what we are to do, to be the example of what he would do today. I can count of many times that I have walked by the homeless sitting on a bench. But I can also count the times that I stopped and sat and ate lunch with them too! Ate a doughnut and drank a cup of coffee on a cold morning! So many times we have opportunity after opportunity to be the hands and feet of Jesus! A simple act of kindness that would make someone's day a brighter day.

Leave Footprints of Love and Kindness Wherever You Go

I want to bless at least one person a week throughout this year in 2021. The other day I was able to bless a total stranger. I was in a local Walmart when I approached a lady who was in the same checkout line that I was in. I asked her if I could bless her with a gift card to help pay for the items in her shopping cart. I loved the feeling that it gave me to be able to help her. This is what I want to do in becoming a better me this new year. Becoming kinder can start at any time, but today would be a great time to start. We need it so badly in our society today. We need kind hearts in the streets. We need kindness in the workplace, in our schools, and in the government. We need it in our churches and, most importantly, in our homes. I challenge you today to do your part to spread kindness wherever you go. One act of kindness at a time will change the world! I have already mentioned her earlier, but my friend Connie Flickinger is truly one of the kindest people I have ever had the pleasure of meeting. I have known her since around 2007, my first year of volunteering with Habitat for Humanity. She volunteered with her church, and we were both on the Faith in Action committee. I honestly believe that kindness is contagious. When you associate yourself with kind, giving people, people who love to serve, their love for serving rubs off on you. Connie is one of those people who gives you all she has literally. I just love being around her and her caring spirit. It has truly made me a better person. She has been a huge influence in my personal life when it comes to serving others. In this world today, people just need to know that someone cares, that someone is there to help when they need it. I meet so many people that are so giving of themselves in my line of work. I have made so many friends also. I love knowing that lives are being changed daily because of them. Kindness cost nothing. It takes zero talent to be kind to one another. I truly believe that we can change the world with kindness. This certainly would make a great start. We have this opportunity each day. We can express kindness to those around us in small ways, and believe me, everyone we meet needs kindness, every hurting soul needs someone to be kind to them. Kindness brings on respect and dignity, along with integrity. These are traits expressed through our acts of kindness. Kind people are my type of people. I have made friends with kind people through my years of volunteering, people that I have met through giving back.

Every now and then I have read a story of kids doing great acts of kindness in their communities. What an awesome and amazing feat! Young minds that have this character in them at a young age. That is just plain good parenting in the home. Kindness is taught. It is learned. It is seen by example from people like you and me. Kindness is needed today more than ever!

Be kind
Be honest
Be loving
Be true
And all of these things
Will come back to you.

Good things will follow you because of your kindness toward others, things like blessings and rewards in life. I truly believe with all my heart that my life has been blessed to the fullest when I have expressed kindness to others. Daddy was always right. He would say to always help others, especially when they needed it the most, during difficult times, times of crisis. I was able to see him express kindness many times in my early childhood life. If someone is hurting and going through a rough time, even a loaf of bread given with love is help to them, he would say to me. I had the pleasure or the honor of seeing him help so many people who were going through rough times in their lives.

Let's stop and take time to look back at a time when you could have shown kindness but chose not to. If you are like me, you have had many opportunities but did not act on them. I know for me I have had these chances but simply did not show kindness. Looking back, I wish I had. Thinking back, I could have made a difference, and someone could have been blessed by kindness. That is ultimately what kindness is all about—blessing others, being a blessing to someone else, something that is beautiful and much needed today. Who will you bless today? Who will receive your kindness today?

Becoming greater requires kindness. You have this within you. Today is the day that you move toward being a better version of yourself with kindness in your heart for others! Kindness will cure many of the problems of the world, simple acts of being kind. I have witnessed in my life, even Christians who profess to know Christ, not being kind to people at times! Do your part to change the world by simply becoming kind. I will certainly work on doing my part. I realize that I must improve in this area as well. It cost nothing to be kind to others. Kindness is a state of mind and heart. I have witnessed many times people being so rude and mean and say to myself, "That was totally not called for!" That person did not deserve to be treated that way. People will show you what is in their hearts by the way they treat you and others. Kind people are a rare breed in our society today. At least, this is what I hear a lot. Do you hear this as well? Sometimes I tend to agree with this; other times, I just believe that I will do all that I can do on my part to spread kindness all around me. At the end of the day, this is all we can do, right? Each day we wake up with this one goal in mind: today I am going to be kind to others! Today I will do my part to make this world a better and kinder world. My community will be kind because of me. My home will be kinder because of me! Let's look at this last statement for a minute. Everything starts at home! I truly believe what is taught at home expands out into the world, into your community. Kindness is taught at home. Being grateful is taught at home. At least, it was when I was growing up and when my kids were growing up. When Daddy wanted me to know something he had to teach me, he set aside time to talk with me. Take time, make time to set aside to talk with your children. This too is a part of becoming greater as we journey toward the pathway to greatness!

Life lesson from this chapter:

If I am going to be greater, I must learn to practice kindness more with those people around me. My goal is to be kinder each day and to spread kindness everywhere!

Make Up Your Mind

This sounds much easier than done. Make up your mind! We have heard this said all our lives. You and I both have had someone say this to us. I believe there is a time when the light comes on. There comes a time when today is the day, my new beginning starts now! As the saying goes, "One day, or day one." We put off so much. I am guilty of that myself many times, of not following through. Getting started is the challenge! When will I start? How will I get going? When will it be the right time? These are all questions that we struggle with and make excuses for. Making up your mind is the starting point. Getting a ready mindset will get you moving toward starting. Think about all the things that can be accomplished with a made-up mind! Maybe a college degree, the opening of a new business venture, a career change, or maybe the writing of your first book and having it published! The possibilities are endless. All that is needed is a mindset that is ready to get started. Make up your mind to be better than yesterday. Sounds simple right! Today might be the day that you get moving. Today might be the day that your mind is made up and a new you begins! I have had so many things that I wanted to do in life. I never had anything more that I wanted to accomplish than to receive my college degree. I enrolled in school a few years after my open-heart surgery in 2009. That event in my life really opened up my eyes to so many things. First of all, that life is short. I was forty-seven years old and could have easily not survived the surgery. After sitting at home recovering from my open-heart surgery, I had eight weeks at home to think. I thought about things that I wanted to accomplish but never did. Getting a college degree was one of them. I am a huge fan and supporter of online school. I am a proud University of Phoenix alumni here, class of 2016. Online school gave me the opportunity to work full-time and attend school full-time as well. Someone may be reading this at this moment, and you have thought about getting that degree. Make up your mind. Go for it. Think about it. You have more years behind you than in front of you if you're my age or older! Even if you are young, you aren't getting any younger! Time is passing us by. Each day is one day wasted when you did not move forward on a dream, a goal, a plan to achieve something in life. I have learned that there is no such thing as waiting until the right time in life. The right time is *now*! There is no better time to make up your mind like the present time. Now is that time. We all wait for the perfect time. There is no such thing. If you are living and breathing, you can make things happen right now.

Someone is waiting for the right time for a career move. You are stuck in a job that you hate, you can't stand being there, but you are afraid to move. You have talked yourself into staying so many times. I know that feeling too. If anyone reading this is like me, I can literally talk myself out of doing anything. Most people are the same as well. I have killed my dreams and plans many times in life. You know all the common excuses: bad timing, not enough money, I am not smart enough, many others. The light finally comes on. The time is now, and you move with a made-up mind! A made-up mind will get you to place that you've never been before. Remember that nothing happens in your life that is beneficial to you, unless you make the move. Moving requires action. Action requires making up your mind to do so!

You are not stuck where you are, unless you decide to be. (Wayne W. Dyer)

Motivation to Move

What gets you motivated to move? Motivation can come in many forms. Usually for me, it is watching someone do something great. I can listen to a great Ted Talk, and I will immediately want to go out and do something that is amazing and gratifying, like helping someone in need or posting a positive message on social media, sharing a quote with my work teammates. I can be motivated in so many ways, but for me my biggest motivation comes from learning about the lives of others, reading and hearing a great story about someone who has done great things in his or her community. This always motivates me to move in the direction of wanting to make life better for someone else. I love to volunteer and suggest volunteering as much as possible to the people around me. Volunteering, in my opinion, puts you in the position where you want to help; and it doesn't matter what you want me to do, I am here for you! I don't hold any position when I help volunteering; I am here to give of myself, my talent, and my time.

It's a beautiful thing when people make up their minds to come together for a greater cause, to fill a certain need. Homes get built, families get fed and clothed, communities come together and take care of the homeless and less fortunate. I think it's safe to say that made-up minds get things done! As I have mentioned, this book is written during the year of the pandemic. The year 2020 has been quite the year. I have seen local people come together and cancel homelessness during these times of COVID-19. People have stepped up and paid for motel rooms for homeless people just to keep them safe and off the streets during the pandemic. One year later and they are still doing it. A local church is feeding families every Friday since the pandemic started almost a year ago. This church is giving out fresh vegetables and fruits, milk and breads weekly to anyone who is in need. I have known the lady behind it, although she would never take full credit for it, but Connie is someone motivated to help, and she will always be right in the middle of seeing things get done and get done right. Motivation to move also takes heart. It takes a special kind of person to want to help others. While wanting to help is a start, rolling up your sleeves ready to go to work is another! It's called action. Not everyone has the heart in them to go to the frontlines. I have always said writing the check is the easy part but going to the street to where the homeless live and being among them like one of them is another thing. What are you willing to do for someone else that will require a made-up mind? Motivation can come in many forms and from many places, most of the time from unlikely places.

Sometimes the worst things that happen in our lives puts us on the path to the best things that will ever happen to us. (Unknown)

A made-up mind takes discipline. It takes heart. Every day we can make things happen. You are the one! Remember the person in the mirror we mentioned earlier? It is that person who can either make something happen or not. You hold the keys that will unlock your potential today. I recall when I was young, maybe preteens, my dad would ask me every day, "What did you learn new today?" As a young kid, it was not always easy to respond with an answer, but even as an adult, can you really think of something new that you learned today? Life is a lesson. We are constantly living and learning about the people that are around us daily. Life is always teaching. During this pandemic, we are all learning more about ourselves, our family, and our friends. We are learning that life is precious. I know I have said that several times already, but never has there been a time when that statement is so true. We are losing friendships over petty things while people are dying each day because of the pandemic. We need to make up our minds to love again. Make up your mind to love those who have caused you pain, especially those who are close to you like a family member or friend. I don't know of anyone who can live with hatred and malice in their hearts. In my opinion, that is not living.

We are seeing the effects of hatred every day in the news that's happening in our country. Hate groups are on the rise. I keep wondering, *When does the light come on in the minds and hearts of people and they start loving people again?* That will certainly take a made-up mind. I will make my mind up in my heart to love those around me, especially those who are different than me. Anything and everything is possible with a made-up mind. My mind is made up to love even when it's not easy, and many times it's not so easy to do so. As I am writing this, I am reminded of something that I did just the other day. I made up my mind to start something new for this new year.

I was inspired by a friend, my friend Connie. She recently gave me four gift cards to give away to random families that I knew could use some help. I was very moved by her kind gesture and decided to do the same, so I purchased some gift cards to have on hand all the time to pass out to random strangers, my way of blessing them. I also have been so motivated this new year with ideas of blessing others that I also was blessed with the opportunity to pay for someone's utility bill, again a random stranger who was in need. I am excited about becoming better at me! When your mind is made up to grow as a person, many things come to mind that you can work on at becoming a better version of yourself. In the process, the people who are around you become blessed too. They get a better person in you to be around. Everyone wins!

I don't write about the acts of kindness that I did to brag on myself but to inspire others to reach out to those who are hurting, to help someone who is struggling in the current moment and needs a helping hand. We have all been there before. I know I have had my days in that situation. My occupation is case manager for a local nonprofit, Methodist Children's Home. My job is to help families with resources that will help them better their lives and be successful. I get to do what I love, helping others, daily. For me, this comes naturally. So I take it a step further in my personal life. Helping continues when I am off the clock as well. I love the statement we have all seen or heard before: "Give and it will return to you." I know this to be so true in my personal life. I want challenge you today to do the same, to become a better version of yourself, serving others and helping those around you. The world needs the best you that you can possibly be! It's time to make our minds to be better than our old selves. We have so much great work to be done in our communities, in your workplace and in our homes. We must make up our minds and get busy! Since my last book, *The Silent Dreamer*, I have changed jobs. I remain in the nonprofit sector, the social workers' world, with a new organization, Methodist Children's Home. This organization has been providing hope for its clients and families for over 130 years. They have offices in states of Texas and New Mexico, providing resources and support and strengthening families and children.

I love working for this organization, and I love the team members in my office. At the end of the day, we all want to see our families succeed in all areas of their lives. I work with families who are committed to making changes in order to be successful in life. There is so much hope and potential to the mind that is made up to want to do better in life. I see this daily with my clients. A made-up mind that is ready for change can have so many doors open for them. The possibilities are endless. You can go from thinking about doing, to making things happen overnight! What will you make up in your mind to start doing today? Will it be the start of a new career? Maybe it's a book you've been wanting to write, or could it be volunteering at the local food distribution? Whatever it is, the time to make up your mind is now! No need to put off what you have made excuses for. For me personally, it could be the day that I give up soda pops! Maybe today is the day that I give those up! A made-up mind gets things done and so does hard work. I have had the pleasure of working or knowing people who are real game changers, people with made-up minds, and they are making this world a much better place to live. Change requires this to take place in our lives. We must make up in our minds in order to make change and to accept change.

It all begins and ends in your mind.
What you give power to has power over you,
If you allow it.

Since writing my first book, *The Silent Dreamer*, I have had so many people mention to me how they have always wanted to write a book. People that have put thought into it but just never took that extra step to make their dream happen. Today just might be your day to make up your mind to follow through on your dreams. If writing a book is something you are interested in, make it happen. For years I believed that money kept me from accomplishing things in life. Money does play a role. It does take money to make things happen. But more than anything, it takes a made-up mind! It takes motivation and drive, the willingness to move forward no matter what obstacles or roadblocks you may encounter in life. For years, my beliefs were that only people with money went to college. School was certainly something that I knew I could not afford. Thank God for financial aid and grants! There is always a way to do something if you want it bad enough. There will always be other options available if you want to accomplish your goals and dreams, but most of all, it takes having a made-up mind. It takes persistence. A changed mind can accomplish anything you set out to do. I feel this way each day. Looking back at my own life, I can see that I am where I am because of the decisions that I made and the support of people who love and believe in me and, most of all, the hand of God on my life! *The Silent Dreamer* would have never happened if a friend had not believed in me and pushed me to write. I never envisioned myself as a writer, but here I am working on my second book project.

What will you make up your mind to accomplish today? Life is short, and let's be honest, we aren't getting any younger. Each day that goes by is another day lost. The time is now. This is the time to get busy with your goals and plans in life. I have started things that did not get finished. Looking back, I have no regrets. My accomplishments have come when it was the right timing. They will for you as well. My accomplishments and goals have also come when my mind was made up to move forward, no more excuses despite the obstacles in place. My mind was made up to proceed and move toward making something happen. When I enrolled in college, there were some people who sent out negative energy in my presence. They did not and could not realize why I would put myself through being a college student at my age. I could have listened to them and dropped out, and once again, I would have quit at something that I had started like many times before. My daughter has a master's degree and working on a second masters. My son just completed his bachelor's degree while working full-time. These two have displayed what it means to make up your mind and go after what you want in life.

If you want something bad enough, you will go after it. If you are hungry enough, you will feed your dreams! You will make up your mind and start working on what you have always dreamed about having in your life. As I mentioned earlier, money is important, but a made-up mind is even more important. It is having the will and desire to accomplish plans and goals. Made-up minds seek greater things in life. Nothing to do with money and fame, they seek to be better people living in this world filled with so much hate. They seek to become the great person that God intended them to be. Again, what will you make up your mind to accomplish today? Someone who is reading this at this very moment is at the crossroads of making up their minds to start something new today, or maybe they are to the point of ending something old, but today is your day to make up your mind! Today is the day to make your dreams come true. Your pathway to greatness begins today with simply making up your mind!

I changed my thinking.
It changed my life.
(Unknown)

Life lesson from this chapter:

Make up in your mind to feed your dreams, plans, and goals in life. Be hungry to accomplish them. Today is the day you make up your mind. Not tomorrow, but today! Mindset is everything!

Why Not You!
Why Not Now!

When will the timing be exactly right? When will it be a great time to start? If you are like me, you have talked yourself down many times. I can honestly say that I am my biggest critic. I believe when you do not have confidence in yourself, that's how it is. One thing that I have learned in recent years is that you must believe in yourself. Like I mentioned in the first chapter in this book, you were made to be great! You were made to succeed in life! Remember, you were created in the image of the Highest God! The time is right now for you. It is your time to shine! You are the star of your own show! You have spent a lifetime watching others succeed and do great things, and you have wondered, *Why not me?* You have wondered when will it be your turn? Your time is now! The circumstances may not be in your favor, but this is your time. I have heard all about bad timing all of my life. The odds are always not in your favor. I can relate to that. I know that feeling. Your future looks much better than your past. Now is the time to rise! With God on your side, you are set to win. You are made for success. I have mentioned in my writings as well as in my first book my struggles with growing up with a low self-esteem. When you have that battle to fight, you don't really feel like a winner. You certainly don't feel like success. What changed my outlook, you might ask? When did I realize that success was made for me as well, that I am worthy! For me, as I got older, I started to believe in myself more and more. Once I graduated from college, I knew that nothing was impossible for me. I wrote about my college journey in my first book, *The Silent Dreamer*. If you knew my entire story, you would see that I put in much work to achieve that accomplishment. My daughter, Tanisha, recently received her master's degree in psychology, a full-time employee, and wife and mother of two kids! My son, Johnny, is currently pursuing his degree also. He is working full-time and doing school. I am so proud of them both. People are doing this every day. They are putting in the work and making things happen, right now! Your time is now as well. You were made for this, so was I. Growing up from the cotton fields, no one told you that you could do great things, no one ever told me anything that would motivate me. Poverty has a way of stripping you from any thoughts of *Why not me! Why not now!* You never feel that it's your time or it's your turn when you grow up poor. Growing up on that farm, I never knew of anytime that I felt it was turn or my time. All I ever did was just want a life away from no running water. The simple things, right?

There is no better time than the present time! We have heard this saying all of our lives. We can try or years later regret we never tried! I know that story all too well. Living with regrets is not easy. My college journey would have never happened if I had just waited on perfect timing. The thing about time is that it doesn't stand still. Time moves on even when we don't! You and I are getting older each day. No matter how we might try to stop it or slow it down, time keeps moving right along. Time is not going to wait for perfect circumstances; it will not wait for the right finances to be in place. You make up your mind, and you move now! I have learned that things will fall right in to place once you make the first move. Don't get me wrong, it takes planning. You set a goal and a date, but the main thing is that you start.

> **Say to yourself**
> **every day:**
> **I love, respect,**
> **accept, esteem,**
> **trust, and believe in me.**
> **I was made for success!**

Here is a small piece of advice: anytime there is something that will benefit you, make you better at what you already do, go for it! Never talk yourself down about making you better! Slow progress is better than no progress! It takes small steps at times, but the key is to keep moving forward! Your time is *now*! I recently talked with a client at work who was interested in getting her high school diploma. She was forty-one years old. I told her my story. I shared with her about how I got my high school diploma at the age of thirty-two years old. I share this story in my first book, *The Silent Dreamer*. I shared with my client how she should pursue this goal and how it would better her life as well as set an example for her children, seeing their mom study to obtain this accomplishment in her life. The work will be hard but the results priceless! Anything worth having in life takes hard work. You have to put the time in. Many people throughout the world are working full-time during the day and studying hard every night. I was one of those people. If you want something bad enough, you put in the work and you make sacrifices. To this day, one of my greatest accomplishments is receiving my high school diploma. Not a big deal to most people but a big deal for me! You and I were made to achieve great things in life, even the small things are paving the way for greater things. Twenty years later I would receive my bachelor's degree. It would lead to my journey in the social work field, moving forward to the publishing of my first book. I truly feel that God is not done with me yet, and he is not done with you, whoever is reading this. He has more plans for you too. Consider this your nudge, that push you've been needing to pursue something in life you have been putting off. You may have even talked yourself out of it too. The time is now to move, and you are the one made for it. Why not you? As I write this, I am considering pursuing my master's degree, something that I started years ago but did not complete. Yes, I am thinking too, *Why not me! Why not now!* I recall when I graduated with my bachelor's degree in 2016, in San Antonio, Texas, I had the honor of being in the company of a mother and son who were also walking the stage that day. These two were recognized for their determination and how they held each other accountable during this journey. They both made it. You can too! What if I fail? What if I don't get the job? What if they don't like me? What if I am not smart enough? These are all excuses you've heard before. I have heard them too and used them too! But what if you don't even try? What if you don't try and you will never know the outcome?

Failure is not in falling down, it is in not getting up again. (Unknown)

Failure is found in simply not trying at all. When you don't try, you've already failed!

I am guilty of this so many times in my life. Countless times I have said, "This is not for me." I have had jobs that I did not apply for because I talked myself out of it. If this sounds familiar to you, *stop doing this*! If anyone is going to tell you that you don't fit the position, let the person interviewing you tell you. Thank them and move on to the next. I have learned that not every door will be open for me, but I never stop believing in myself. Never stop turning doorknobs! Your door is out there. Your story is not done yet. You still have plan and purpose. God promises us this: before we were even born, he had a plan and purpose for you and I, to prosper us, to give us hope and a future. I love the fact that it took me years to realize that I am worthy of good things happening to me. I want to take the time to share with you the same news: you are worthy too! I know you feel like nothing never good happens to you, but today is the day that changes. You were made for great things; you were made to succeed and to be the head and not the tail. Believe that good things are coming your way. It's your turn; it's your time. I recall years ago I came home upset about a promotion that someone else had gotten at work. To this day I am not sure why I was so mad. I didn't even apply for the job. Why would I be so mad about a job that I did not even apply for? The reason that I did not apply was because I thought I was not qualified for the position. Looking back years later, maybe I was upset with the fact that I thought so little of myself, feeling not worthy of even applying. So many questions loom when we don't believe in ourselves. Like I mentioned earlier, I have talked myself out of so many things in my life simply for just not feeling like it's my time, this is not for me, or I am not qualified. Friends, let me tell you, you are made for this moment. You are smart enough. You are good enough for this opportunity. Now is your time! It sounds simple, but it's not that easy. Trust me, I understand. You got to believe in yourself. You and I have heard this all our lives, well, maybe not all our lives; but at some point and time, we have had someone tell us to believe, just believe. If only I had followed through on that goal, I have had this statement play many times in my mind. Countless times I just did not act on something because I just felt this is not for me. Those days are behind me! I feel that I can accomplish anything I set my mind to do. I want you to feel the same way. You are good enough, you are smart enough, and you were made for this very moment in your life. There has never been a better time than *now*! These are affirmation statements that you should say to yourself every day and often. This is my time! This is my turn! Say it loud that your ears hear what your mouth is saying. Say this while you are driving. Say it throughout the day to yourself. Say it loud if you must say it. Learn to become who you were really meant to be. You are the star of your very own show. No one can play your role but you. You have prayed for this opportunity; you have worked hard to be where you are. This is your moment. I know people who have worked so hard to be in the position they are in. Some have started from the very bottom and worked their way up through the ranks, years of hard work, tears of disappointment; but here they are, doing great things. It's finally their time. My daughter is one of those people. She was a young mother, going to school and working at the same time, obtaining her associates degree from a local small junior college and raising my grandson as well. A student, a mother and working full-time—what we would call a full plate. If this sounds familiar, maybe because this is you, reader. People are doing this every day, juggling life and working toward their dreams at the same time. I did the same thing not that long ago, and I am not done yet. I know without a doubt that God has so much more for me to do in life, both professionally and personally. He has so much more for you to do as well. You may have come to a fork in the road, but trust in His timing and seek His will. He will direct you. At the end of the day, it all comes down to trusting Him. He knows what is best for us. Ask God for big things, and you will get big results!

Think big and dream bigger! You have all the tools within you to do great things; and most of all, with a great support system, you are unstoppable. I had the pleasure of speaking to someone who had recently purchased my first book, *The Silent Dreamer*. This lady shared with me how my book inspired her, and she wanted to let me know that she had purchased three more copies to give as gifts. I shared with her that I had many people in my life that helped me and supported me along the way. Thinking back, I look at the years when I was enrolled in online college courses, working all day and studying almost all night, at least if felt like it! That was my time, and I made the most of it. It's your time, and you need to make the most of it right now! Opportunities present themselves, but they will not always be there for you. Seize the moment. We have always heard, take advantage of moment right now. Dreams and goals come true only when you put in the work. I know people who have done great things and are currently doing amazing things and making contributions to their communities. We would call them a success. What we fail to see or recognize is the hard work that it took for them to get there. We don't see the tears and sweat that was poured out to get there. There is a cost. It's called hard work and determination.

My dad taught me many things. Working for what you want in life was on the top of the list. Daddy would say, "Work using your head more than your hands!" Don't get me wrong, there is nothing wrong with hard work. Working your fingers to the bone, your hands and feet tired at the end of the day—I know all about that. Been there and done that for most of my life. My dad was one of those people, a hardworking man who knew hard work. Most men of his era knew hard work as well. Working in the cotton fields as a young kid, so did I. What Daddy meant was that, for me, he wanted a better life for me, a much easier life. Like any good father, he wanted the best for his son. I feel the same for my children and for their children. It's good to teach a good work ethic to our children. My son and daughter were taught to work hard, show up and put in a good day's work, be respectful with those around you especially the with the boss. Your character will open or close doors for you!

I know this personally. I had to do something that I have never done in my life: quit a job and return to that very same job a few months later. I knew I could return based on my character and work ethic. I have a good work history everywhere I have been. This will follow you. It can either help you or hurt you. We will talk about this more later in this book. By now, you should be ready to act upon something that you have put off for some time now. I have shared with you moving in the moment. The time is now, and why not you! You deserve success, greatness, rewarded for your hard work and determination. My daughter, who has a master's degree already and pursing another one currently, got a new job recently, a promotion with a local nonprofit. Like her dad, she loves helping others. My daughter interviewed, and they were impressed with her. How would they not be, right? This is my kid! The point that I want to make here is that the fruit doesn't fall far from the tree, as they say. My daughter and I also have worked together before for a local nonprofit, although neither of us are there today. I really learned a lot about her heart for helping people. I have no doubts that she is going to do well at her new job with her new position. This kid is smart and brings new ideas and is open to new ideas. We talk and share a lot of the same concepts, but at the end of the day, all we want is to bless a family and make their lives better. We all win! Winning only happens when you play. The game has to be played in order to declare a winner. You are not only in the game just to play. I want to play and win! Winning comes from all we have covered so far: a made-up mind, a heart of gratitude, being kind to others, and moving in the moment, right now! Today is your day to start winning in life. It is all part of the process of becoming a better version of yourself. Learn to trust the process. Although it might look like things are not in your favor, trust the process, trust His plan for your life. God is not surprised by the obstacles that you face. He is aware of what you are facing in life. The process does not always feel good, but sometimes this is necessary. It gets you out of your comfort zone. I have learned, while trusting in the process, that there is only the current moment to live in. No looking back or looking ahead, but trusting in the current moment. There will never be the right timing. Now is the time! It's your time to get moving on your dreams and plans. The time is now for you to proceed on making things happen in your life. No one can take your place. This moment is just for you and only you! I am so excited about what my future holds. I am excited about the platform my first book has put me on. I was recently having a conversation with a person that I met at a recent book signing event. She was sharing with me about how this is my time! She stated to me that all that I am doing concerning the success of my first book, *The Silent Dreamer*, is all part of my time being right now! I thought about this conversation literally all day. I came to this conclusion: if you help and support the dreams of others, you will eventually live your own dreams! Be patient. Your time will come! This is all part of your destiny for greatness. Trust the process. Your time will come. Stay the course, stay faithful, and stay prayerful!

If you don't have big dreams and goals
You will end up working really
hard for someone who does.

Life lesson from this chapter:

Always trust the process! Things may not look like they are in your favor, but trust the process always! Slow progress is better than no progress!

Your Gift Will Make Room for You!

People spend their lifetime looking for what they like, what they want to be in life. Growing up, I never gave it much thought. I kind of knew the regular stuff, like being a police officer, fireman, and doctor, were all out of the question. Even as a little boy even, I knew that my situation of growing up poor, there was not much of a chance to be any of those occupations. Finding what you like can be a challenge for most people. It is not easy. But then some people are born and know that something is in them that sets them apart. They are gifted, and that gift will make room for them. They know all too well what they like, what they want to do in life. I have known people who knew exactly what they wanted to be in life. They knew their what they liked from an early age. "I always knew that I wanted to be a schoolteacher," says a friend of mine. As a child, the only thing that I knew was that I wanted to leave the farm that I grew up on. I wanted a life that was better than the one I had as a child growing up on that farm. Growing up in poverty makes you so thankful for the little things, for me back then, just indoor plumbing was a luxury! Having indoor plumbing would have been all I needed in life. I have been in the electrical field as an electrician since 1982. This can be called my gift. I fix things, install lighting and outlets, etc. I am blessed to be in this field of work. Again, growing up, I never said ever that I want to do electrical work for a living. I got in this field because of my dad and my cousin who were working in the electrical field for a local electrical contractor.

Ask yourself, What am I good at? What makes me happy? What is rewarding to me? Let's not confuse your gift with your occupation. We all must work to make a living. My dad told me years ago, if I learned a trade, I would always have a job. He was correct. I can do electrical work anywhere I want to. I am good at what I do. I say that as humble as I can. I am simply stating that I have learned from the best in the field. I love this trade that I learned many years ago. My cousin Roy taught me so much, and I had others who took me under their wing.

Your gift will make room for you. This is scripture. What you know will open doors for you. Everyone is gifted. Not one single person on this earth is without a gift. We all have something that we are good at, passionate about, something that drives us and makes us who we are. That gift defines us. I mentioned earlier about a friend who will help anyone. She will literally give of herself. Her passion is to help; her gift is to help others. I would say my gift and passion is helping others as well. This is something that I discovered years ago. You have a gift as well, whether you realize it or not. Your gift will drive you; it will keep you up at night. Your gift will inspire you to continue even when you want to throw in the towel. What I have learned in life is this: if it is your gift and passion, your gift will find you! You will not have to look for it; it will find you! And once you find it, you groom it, you improve it, you make your gift better and better each day. My trade as an electrician is something that I do. It's made me an honest and decent living for the most part of my adult life. Even today I still do work for myself. It's my part-time business. But my gift is to help others. My gift is to make a difference in the lives of the people that I am around daily. My degree was to be in a field where I could do just that, help people. I prayed for that many times. "Lord, put me in the position where I can make a difference." I think of this often as I am driving to the office. I love helping people; that is my passion. I am driven to do this. What drives you? What have you discovered about yourself? What is your gift to your community? What is your gift to those around you each day? What about your gift to the world? Let's focus on this. Your gift will make room for you! This is scripture and stands so true. Our gifts will open doors and lead us in the direction we should go in life.

I was recently on a walk with my dog, Thor. I recalled when I was growing up how my uncle Bennie could build anything. My uncle had no education. He could not read and nor write, but he always was good at math! At least, the part that counted like keeping track of his work hours and figuring out his paycheck! That is amazing. How does one do this? You could give him two numbers, and he could add it up in his head! Like I mentioned, he could build anything. This was obviously his gift. Everyone is gifted, even the uneducated. Your gift does not require an education, does not require a degree. What is required is your heart. My uncle Bennie put heart into his gift. He would help anyone who needed help building something. Uncle Bennie also had a green thumb. He could grow anything from peanuts to watermelons! He loved his gardens. He put his heart into those plants. Every seed that was sown produced something. Life should be the same way. Our gifts should be the same. We sow into people, and in turn, they reap what we have poured into them from the use of our gifts. I see this daily on my job. I sow a seed into my client. Maybe it's a resource that they stand in need of, maybe it's helping with picking up food, or any other need for them; but nonetheless, it's a seed that meets a need! Use your gift to plant seeds today. You are needed for this very reason. I have said this for most of my adult life. I love helping people! Most people who know me, and know me well, already know this about me. I am driven by that. I am not surprised that I am in the field that I have chosen to pursue for my life career, social work field. I have no doubt this is where God wants me to be. If I have one weakness, it is that I do not know how to say *no*! I am the ultimate people pleaser. This is a life lesson that I am still in class learning. I am not saying this like it's a bad thing, but people will take advantage of you. I have had my share of this. I have often said that if I won the lottery, I would give it all away! Well, at least most of it! On a serious note, I would help so many people and organizations that I am so fond of. Like I said earlier, my biggest weakness is that I cannot say *no*! A topic we will cover later in this book. I truly believe that you can find your gift by being around gifted people. People who show their gifts daily, people who live their gifts before their very eyes.

I cannot believe that I have not mentioned a lifelong friend of mine. We have been friends since 1994. That year I went to work for a textile company that is no longer in the Brenham, Texas, area, Mount Vernon Mills. I met a guy there who was an electrician for the plant. His name was Donald Guyton but goes by the name Tank. To this day I know him and call him Tank. This guy became more than just a fellow coworker; he became a brother. Let me introduce you to my friend Tank. He is very much into details. When he does a job, it's going to be done right and look even better. Not that I never was much on details and looks before, but I developed an eye for this just by being around Tank daily.

"Do you want your name on that?" I catch myself saying that to myself all the time. "Johnny, do you want your name on that?" After all, we do live in a society where looks define us, even when it comes to an electrical project. My friend Tank can build anything. He can cook anything. To this day, he has the best barbeque that I have ever tasted! It is safe to say that Tank has many gifts. He wears many hats: electrician, carpenter, cook. Did I mention he is a mechanic as well? I have never known anything Tank does not have some knowledge on. He is truly gifted plumber, HVAC man—the gifts keep growing as I write this! You can see that my friend is someone I am very partial to. He has helped me and others countless times. Although Tank is gifted in all these areas that I mentioned and more, his gift comes from his heart. Remember earlier I mentioned about how our gift is found in our hearts. He has the heart to help others with his gifts. One of the kindest people that I know, he is giving, he is helpful, he is a loyal friend of mine. I can honestly say that his gifts have rubbed off on me. As the word of God says, iron sharpens iron! We become who we associate ourselves with! Read that again. The word of God says that bad company ruins good morals. This is found in 1 Corinthians 15:33 (KJV). Let's be clear on something. This does not mean that people can be bad. They may very well be good people, great friends; but when their views cause you to change and conform to theirs, you guessed it, you have changed and may not even realize it at the time.

But I have seen this happen in the opposite way. You can conform to their ways if they are positive, loving, giving, and gifted!

Finding your gift is something that you may work toward for many years, or you find it sooner than later. Some may even be born with it. Your gift will define who you are as a human being. We will be remembered long after we are gone by our deeds and works. People will talk about our legacy long after we leave this earth. I don't know about you, but I want people to remember me by my acts of kindness and my gift of what I have done to help others. Some people may say, it does not matter to me what others think of me after I am gone. It matters to me. It matters that my children and grandchildren know that their grandfather left a legacy that they can be proud of. It should matter to you as well. My father has been gone over thirty-five years, and I still remember his good works for helping others. His lessons in life are still fresh in my mind. I miss him dearly and miss him daily. I often think of how Daddy would be so proud of me today, but to be honest, he was proud of me when I thought I wasn't much of anything. Daddy always believed in me, and I knew this. No matter how many times I thought that I had failed, he always believed in me and was proud of me. In his eyes, my gift would take me places eventually. And it has! Whether I am doing electrical work or signing a book for someone, Daddy would be so proud of his only son. Yes! Your gift will pave a way for you. It will place you where you need to be in life, the right job in the right field of work with the right people you need to be with.

Do good for others. It will come back to you in unexpected ways. (Unknown)

The gift that you have was meant to be shared with others. People should benefit from your gift. Someone should reap from the seed that is sown with your gift. People bless others with their gifts. They nourish and flourish others with what they have been gifted with. I have the honor of working each day with a team of people who use their gifts in helping others, team members who bring to the table lots of years of experience of helping the clients that we serve working with clients from all walks of life. I love the people I have met in my field of work, so many inspiring people who love what they do and use their gifts each day. People who work with youth, the elderly, veterans, the homeless, the victims of domestic violence, the unemployed and underemployed, the many people that are hurting and are in a hard place in life. I have met so many people who love what they do for a living, and they are good at what they do. They are gifted. Your gift will inspire others to use their gifts. This is what I love about volunteering. Volunteering is another area in which people use their gifts, whether it's building a house with Habitat for Humanity or delivering meals in your community to the less fortunate. Use your gift to bless others.

Life lesson from this chapter:

Use your gift to bless others! Use your gift to inspire others for change! Your gift will make room for you! Your gifts will open doors for you! Everyone has a gift!

Learn to Say No!

If you want more time, freedom and energy, start saying *no*.

—Unknown

I can think of a thousand times when I wished I had said no, how my life would be so different if I had just said no. I mentioned earlier that I am a people pleaser. I find it very difficult to say no, even when in my mind and heart I truly want to. Maybe you are like me as well. We both make it a habit of not knowing how to say this small word. We are both afraid that we will let someone down, and that is simply not what we are wired to do. To be honest, I have struggled with this as a kid growing up. I felt as a kid growing up that if I said yes to everything, I would be liked. I avoided conflict as I grew older. If I said yes, this would prevent an argument. I would keep and make friends. Boy, this really came back to haunt me. As I grew older, I realized more that I can say no and not have to explain myself. I have been an electrician for over thirty-five years now. As I get older, there are certain types of service calls that I just don't want to do anymore because of my age and the well-being of my body. It has taken me so long to just say no when I don't want to do certain jobs. "Just say no and don't feel bad about it," I keep saying to myself.

I am probably not alone in this area. Saying no can feel like you are letting others down. I have felt that way many times, but what about yourself? Aren't you letting yourself down by pleasing others when you simply wished you had just said no and moved on. I am also the first to say "I am sorry." This is another sign of a people pleaser, always the first to want to make things right. I have found myself in this position many times even when I was the one who got hurt. The peacemaker, that's what I am, the one who would rather take the blame than to have someone mad or upset. I can say that this part of me goes way back to middle school grade when I was being bullied by a girl on my school bus. I was probably in the sixth grade, tall, skinny kid, Afro, and afraid of almost anything. If you said boo, I would have jumped out of my skin! I was never a fighter. I have never been in a fight my entire life. Who would fight me and why? Fighting is simply not in my DNA.

"Why would anyone not like me?" I asked myself all the time as a quiet kid. Who would have a problem with me? I have discovered in life that people can and will dislike you regardless of how nice or how good you have been to them. When you are a people pleaser and peacemaker, they do not need to have a reason. All of this goes with not being able to say no! In my opinion, I have always felt that people see me as a weak person. I show a lot of emotions, someone who is very emotional. I wear my emotions on my sleeves. Like I mentioned earlier, I am not sure what I ever did to be bullied on the bus. I know that as a kid I found it to be very frustrating! I think that as a kid, my life was setting me up for what it would be as an adult. I needed to set up boundaries even then, part of saying no to this person who was bullying me. When you don't like something, just say no! You don't have to participate in anything that you don't want to give energy and time to. How many times have you said to yourself, "How I wish I had said no!" If you are like me, you have said it too many times to keep count. But that is what people pleasers do, we do all we can to please others even if it neglects our own well-being. There is nothing wrong with putting you first. Try it sometime. For once put yourself before others. This feeling is amazing! As people pleasers, we value so much in making others happy, making sure that others are not upset with us that we neglect ourselves. Let me be the first to say that this is a life lesson. I am daily learning this lesson. I recently read this amazing quote. It read, "If you are a giver, please know your limits cause the takers don't have any." This statement is so true, and something that I have had to learn throughout the years. You can literally drain yourself of giving so much of yourself. If you are like me, you have probably wondered, *Why do I give a damn so much?* And like me, friend, you and I are just wired that way. It's in your DNA. You care for people who would not lift a finger to help you if you needed it. I think we can agree, with saying no comes with boundaries. I recall years ago having a friend tell me, "Johnny, you cannot save the world. You cannot do it all by yourself. You have to say no sometimes." Rest in peace my dear friend, Alice. I remember our conversation if it was just yesterday. I tend to overwhelm myself with wanting to do so many things and help so many people at the same time. This is something that I have gotten better at over the years. We can only fight small battles one at a time. We can only put out one fire at a time. You and I both owe it to ourselves to put us first! I know from personal experience, I can be overwhelmed by putting others first so any times. God knows there are times I question myself, but I know that the spirit of helping others is part of who I am. The problem with putting out fires is that just when you have one almost put out, another one starts up! There will always be needs to be met, hurting people who need people like you and I. Let's just say that we can limit our nos!

I have learned one priceless piece of advice working in the social work world: take care of yourself! I know this sounds like it's not very eye-opening advice, but it really is. I am learning all the time about taking care of *me* more! If you don't take care of yourself, who will? And you don't have to be in the helping field to get burned out. You can get to this point in your life just with dealing with family matters, coworkers, friends who depend and rely on you for many things on many occasions. Life happens, as the saying goes. Things happen that are out of our control, but we do control how we respond. You are however the master of your emotions, or at least, that is what we are working toward. Saying that small word can be so refreshing. Each time that I have said no has been so wonderful to me, like weight lifted from my shoulders, like freedom. I recently talked on the phone with a former teammate from my old job. She was sharing with me how overwhelmed she felt and how she felt like burnout was coming on. I have learned in this field of work. We give so much of ourselves, we make it a habit to fix problems, and we feel like we are in the position where the last thing a client wants to hear from us are the word *no* said to them. In this field of work, the social work field, we hear this all the time. You cannot pour from an empty cup. In order to help others, you must care for yourself first. In order to do just that, you must be willing to learn to say no at times. I am learning more each day that saying no does not mean that I don't care. It simply means that there are times when I care about me this time, and there is nothing wrong with that. There is not one thing wrong with caring about you first this time. You have earned it; you deserve it! I am learning more and more the importance of self-care, especially during this time of pandemic. We are so devoted to helping and doing for others, health-care workers deemed as essential care workers. I see it daily in the social work field. If you gain anything from this chapter in particular, know that self-care is so vital to your own well-being. This is another reason for learning to say no! Make it a habit to invest in yourself. Make it a habit that you find and do things that bring you happiness. You need to spend time doing something that you enjoy and brings you so much joy you cannot wait to do it. I recently started doing paint by number. One of my coworkers got me hooked on this, and now it's a hobby that I enjoy very much. This is my self-care. This is my time spent relaxing, thinking of what I will write next.

Learning to say no will open other doors for you, other opportunities and experiences. The results are endless. Learn to say no for the sake of your mental health and well-being. Saying no doesn't mean that I don't care, nor does it mean I have no interest; it simply means that this time, I am putting me first! And by doing so, I feel no guilt. This is okay by me. Saying no feels good this time, no pressure, no worries! My life is much better knowing that I can care for myself without feeling bad for putting my self-interest first for a change. Life is short; time is precious. We take so much for granted, and our time is probably taken for granted the most. We spend so much time doing for others we tend to forget about ourselves. I am in the process of taking a weekend off each month, no work, no writing, no book events, just time relaxing, some great overall *me* time! Most people who know me can honestly say that I am a workaholic!

I am never idle, moving and doing something all the time. This new thing about me not working and relaxing is new to me, but I am willing to learn to take time for me and relax. You should as well. Learn to simply say no! Everything does not require your attention. Calm down and relax. Saying no gives you more peace of mind. That alone is so important and priceless. People pleasers like you and I put ourselves last, but that must change, and now is the time for change! The time is now for you and me to get comfortable with saying no and learning to say yes to our peace of mind and self-care. I am learning more as I get older, if you don't learn to say no more, you will be taken advantage of by people who are close to you as well as strangers! People prey on people pleasers. People will knowingly take advantage of you just because of your kindness, unfortunately. Saying no is a gift. We should use it wisely. It is also a form of self-care we should all learn to practice.

> Be there for others, but never leave yourself behind. (Dodinsky)

Life lesson from this chapter:

Learn to say no. This is peace of mind and benefits your mental self-care. It's okay to say no without guilt.
Seven Rules for a Happy Life:

1. Never hate.
2. Give.
3. Forgive and move on.
4. Smile often.
5. Show respect and receive respect.
6. Give some more.
7. Trust God in everything.

If you want to find happiness, find gratitude.

—Steve Maraboli.

Next-Level Thinking

If you are like me, you are at the crossroads of having the best chapter of your life happen right now. You are making changes and moving toward better days ahead. Every decision that you make is making you a better person who is ready for something big to happen that is in your favor. I call this next-level thinking, reaching for bigger and better things. You deserve it. You have earned it. You have worked hard to get to this stage of your life. One thing that I have learned in my life is that you cannot think next level when you are living low-level character. Read that again if you must. This is a lesson I had to learn myself in life. If you want to get to that level, some changes must take place. Let's look at this level in our lives. It takes discipline, the start of some good habits, people who are in your corner, those who encourage you and support your ideas. I have come to notice that not everyone will cheer you on when you do well in life. I have traveled a long road from my life growing up on a former cotton plantation. I have come from lying in bed at night as a young kid dreaming of making something of myself, being success however that would be. God knows I never had a clue what that would even look like. Poverty robs you of so much. It takes you away from what you dream and envision. You feel like that will never happen for me, but you dream anyway.

As a kid growing up in extreme poverty, my next-level thinking took me to indoor plumbing and just a decent place to call home, nothing more. My goals were not big goals that needed much to accomplish. Next-level thinking was far from cotton fields and wanting to get away from them as a kid working in the hot summer heat in Central Texas. I want you to look at what goes on when you think next level but your circumstances, your situation in life keep you from moving up to that level. This type of thinking requires being around people who think bigger than you do. It requires learning from others who push you into being greater than you could ever imagine. These people stretch you beyond your limits. There are certain people who I can talk with and as soon as I am done talking, I am ready to conquer the world! I get inspiration and motivation from just hearing them talk about the good things that are happening in their lives. If a friend of mine is sharing with me about being blessed, I feel blessed as well for them sharing with me. This is how next-level thinking works, being able to share in the excitement of someone else's blessing. I have learned this one thing in my fifty-nine years of living. Not everyone claps when you win; not everyone congratulates you in your success. In my opinion, that hinders next-level thinking. For example, my first book that was published in 2020, *The Silent Dreamer*, I shared information about it on every social media outlet you can imagine. I wanted to get the word out and let others know of what I had just accomplished. Of course, this was a big deal for me. It still is. I also took the liberty of sharing books that some of my author friends had released on my page and website. I wanted others to see what my friends were doing and share in spreading the word about their work. That is just my nature. I can say that I did not get the same response in return, but I am okay with that. My heart and motives were pure. That is all that matters. That is next-level thinking. I know that at the end of the day, I am good with my decisions and choices when it comes to praising others, sharing what they have done, retweeting a post, sharing a picture, buying their books. It's about supporting those around you who are doing what you are doing. I have no doubt that my time will come. I will live my dreams, the dreams from a quiet boy from the cotton plantation. I am living them as I write. I am living each day a dream that no one could have imagined for me. But fear not, I am not done dreaming yet! I am just turning the corner. I believe that what we want the most will take us to the places we need to go the most, and that is time spent with God, praying and talking to him our plans and getting His approval. After all, he has the last word. He orders our steps. I am at the point of my life where all that I want to do is make my name known with others as someone who is a team player. I am just a small-town country boy who made it to where he is by way of going the long route in life. Nothing has come easy. I have had to crawl and scratch my way to get this far in life. I have had every reason to give up and forget about thinking at a higher level. I am driven by what I learned growing up in that small wood-framed house on that cotton plantation. You give it all that you have. You learn to make something out of nothing. This is bigger than making lemonade out of lemons! We are talking old school here, the hustle, the grind—call it what you will. Heck, we didn't even have lemons to make lemonade with! I think it's safe to say that I had next-level thinking even back then as a kid! I learned at an early age that you have to help one another. You have to when you are poor. You need one another. You depend on each other.

I can recall my sweet mother planning meals each day, sewing our clothes, and making sure we had clean clothes to wear. Thinking back, she had so much to do raising us, and she did not have much help in doing so. Living daily was a struggle. The pantry would be empty most days. Next-level thinking requires planning and preparation. You must have a plan in place in order to accomplish what you want to achieve. You must also be prepared to make it to the next level. Planning is all about making plans to succeed. You must get in the mindset to see yourself where you want to be in life. Planning is so vital, whether the goal is big or small. You must plan, write it down on paper, read it daily. I love making my vision board. I love putting pictures with words and having a visual to look at and remember what I have said that I want to achieve, my planning posted on a board. My father, with little to no education, was the ultimate planner. What I would give to read one of his pocket note pads. He would always keep them handy to write things down, making plans come to life, keeping record of important events in life. Those little notebooks were filled with greatness! My father always did things with planning and never at the last minute. It was always calculated out, date and time. Everything would be put into place days, even weeks before something occurred. My father was always thinking ahead. Was he a bit of an overthinker? Maybe you could have called him that, but he was always prepared for the good or bad, another trait of next-level thinking. I recall living in a house that Daddy owned. The house had not one propane gas tank, but three! His belief was to always have more than needed in case of an emergency. He did the same with food. He had a room at his house filled with canned goods and other nonperishable food items. His own food pantry in the house that could have fed the entire block on his street! He was always overprepared, thinking ahead all the time, never being caught off guard. I believe that is how a next-level thinker is to live. Never being caught off guard, always prepared. Yes, Daddy was on to something. I can honestly say that he did his best to teach me this concept, but for a young man having to grow up fast, I did not understand what he was trying to teach me then. Today looking back and much older, I see the importance of this way of thinking. It goes beyond saving for a rainy day; this is a total mindset. It goes beyond just thinking ahead; you must see the greater picture, if it is with saving money, even if it's just putting back a few dollars every paycheck for starters. As I get older, I am now looking what my next move will be, making my next move greater than my last move. This should be your goal as well. It's about winning and doing what it takes to see the results.

Let's take a look at next-level thinking with some specific planning involved. I want to share a personal story involving a five-year plan. I can recall this as if it were yesterday. I was working for the city of Bryan at the time, but I was leaving this job where I had spent twelve years of my life there. I was going to my new gig with Brazos County. I was pumping gas when I got a plan in my head to have a job related to my degree within the next five years. I was in school, the year was 2012, the month was August; but in my mind, I had already called it. "Just five more years," I would say to myself. I am going to work for the county five years, and then I am leaving to pursue a new career with my degree in human services management. I called it; I could see it. I graduated from the University of Phoenix with my degree in February of 2016; and in August of 2017, almost to the date that I had planned to leave the county, I left to pursue my new career in the social work field. You must plan and be clear on what you want. Like mentioned earlier, you must write it down on paper. You have to speak it with your mouth. Next-level thinking requires you to be specific about you want to accomplish in life. I have done this a few times. Trust me, it works! I was specific on the type of job that I wanted. I targeted a few nonprofits in my area, the ones that I wanted to work for, the ones I felt that I could bring what I had to offer in terms of my team-player mentality and being positive in the workplace. I have always said that I want to be the best at what I do! Every day when I show up, you know that I am bringing my best game to the workplace. You can attribute that to next-level thinking. I want to be able to know that I have done my best to help the families that I serve. I have been in the electrical field for over thirty-five years now, and to this day, I feel like I am one of the best who has ever put on a tool belt. I am not speaking like someone who is arrogant. I am just stating that I am good at what I do. Again, it was my dad who talked me into going in that field of work. Another example of next-level thinking on his behalf. Next-level thinking requires you to see things about you that others see. My father saw that I could do more than what I was doing at the time that he wanted me to learn a trade. It is amazing what a person can do when others believe in him or her. The possibilities are limitless. It sounds so simple, but you have to believe in yourself. You have to trust the process. The obstacles that are before you are steppingstones to the next level. You will step over into another realm of where you want to be in life.

Let me remind you that you can do anything that you put your mind to do, anything! I am talking about having vision, seeing yourself in that position, on that job, in that house, in that car! But next-level thinking goes beyond material things. It's about a state of mind! It's about being, finding your purpose in life, and doing what is necessary to get to that place in your life. It all begins and ends with how we think, what we focus on, where we spend our energy. What are you focused on today? Where are your thoughts, and what are you so passionate about that it drives you to thinking to the next level? When you think about this question, it involves much of what has been covered in this book already. It involves having a made-up mind, thinking like a champion, having also a spirit that is giving and kind, just to name a few; but you get the picture. It's all about becoming a great version of yourself.

Next-level thinking is about believing in yourself no matter what the circumstances are. You believe that you can, and you will win! That may sound easy, but it can be a challenge as well. Looking back, I have so much confidence in myself today compared to years ago. I remember long ago, I was doing electrical work for myself. This was during a time when I was out of work. I had gotten laid off from my regular job with a local contractor. Work was slow at the time. I picked up work doing service call work. I had this one customer who was the manager at an apartment complex. This account kept me busy, and I had made an impression with the manager. He really liked my work and called me out to fix electrical problems regularly. This guy was a member of a local group that were in the process at the time of building homes in a local subdivision. They were going to start out with fourteen homes. I recall when this guy presented this opportunity to me, he wasn't looking for bids from other companies; he wanted me to do the electrical wiring of these fourteen starter homes. He was interested in no one else but me! I was, on the other hand, young and broke. I had no resources to even start a project like this. I was literally a one-man show. I had a cousin who was willing to help me, but along with me not having any money, I had no confidence in myself that I could pull this project off. I had no next-level thinking at the time. I have never forgotten this opportunity and the what-ifs that go along with thinking back, wondering what could have been. I have done a lot of electrical work since that time, but an opportunity like that never came around again. I am okay with that, but for someone else, you have had opportunities that slipped by you and wondered what could have happened. We have all lived with regrets. Looking back, the money was not what really kept me from moving forward on that opportunity. It was my mind, my thinking of *I cannot do this, I am not confident of my work.*

If you learn anything from this chapter or even this book, it is to never doubt yourself. Others may have doubts about you, but please do not ever doubt yourself. Always believe in *you*! I am okay with others who do not believe in me; they don't really have to. But

I, on the other hand, must believe in myself. This is a requirement of myself daily. I am not done yet, and you aren't either. We both have so many things to accomplish in life. I know where I want to be. The question is, do you? Where are you when it comes to knowing where you want to be in the current moment, and what will it take for you to get there? These are questions that only you can answer. I can give you all the encouragement you need, the push, the coaching; but you hold the keys. You know what you need to let go, of what changes need to be made in your life. You may need to drop some people out of your circle and maybe add some that will help and not hurt you. Truth be told, people already know who these people are in their lives. It's really no surprise. Make the necessary changes in order to get to next-level thinking.

The journey is all a part of the process. The highs and the lows, the closed doors the doors slammed in our faces—this all part of where we have come from to get where we are going. Obstacles and valleys are all a part of gaining success, being the person that God intended us to be. I have been on both ends, the highs and the lows, the successes and the failures. I can relate very well to both. I think that it is safe to say that next-level thinking also requires being happy in the choices that we make in life. I know that I am my happiest when things are going well, and I am happy with the decisions I have made with no regrets. Life is about being happy and living to be more and more happy as it goes on. This is a life lesson that I am learning daily. At the end of the day, I want to be happy knowing that I am thinking next level with every decision that I have made that day, and I can go to bed happy knowing that I have given the day my very best. I also want those around me to think to the next level as well. I truly feel this can be and should be contagious to those who are around us. This type of thinking requires putting yourself in position to win! "It's not over until I win," says one of my heroes, Les Brown. Always put yourself in position to come out on top. Position is vital to everything we encounter in life. Where are you positioned today?

Next-level thinking also requires being in the circle of those who think like you do. They want the same goals you want. Their plans are similar to your plans. You can both relate. Great minds think alike, it's said. You must have people in your circle who have similar ideas to the ones that you bring to the table, people who want to grow as much as you do, people who want to succeed.

**Don't shrink your goals,
Increase your efforts.**

Life lesson from this chapter:

Next-level thinking requires positioning yourself to win! Get involved with like-minded people, people who want to succeed as well!

Bitter or Better

I have heard this, and so have you. Life can make us either bitter or better. Those are the choices or options that we have, how we respond to circumstances or situations in life. I know for me personally I have had responded to things in my life where I have been both, better and sometimes bitter. My human response at times has been to get even. If someone hurts me, hurt them back in return. Again, this is me just being human. I have learned, and I am currently learning all the time, that happiness is about how we respond to situations in life. We have all experienced things in life where we did not get the answer we were looking for, we did not get the job or promotion we had hoped for. Life is full of setbacks and disappointments. We all experience them. We all must decide if we become bitter or better from them. I have heard all my adult life this saying, "Everything happens for a reason." To be honest, even though that may be true about life, it's not the answer that I always want to hear! Life and people can let us down. Those who say they love us the most can hurt us the most! To be honest, I have only been hurt by people who claim they love me!

Most of us could easily walk around with bitterness in our hearts. We have all been hurt and denied something in life we felt deserving. I know that speaking for myself, I certainly have many times in my life felt this way. Somewhere I have read in scripture not to repay evil with evil, but to repay evil with good and leave revenge in the hands of God. I must believe that this way works out so much better and the results are in His hands and not mine. I have known some people who spend their entire lives bitter over something that happened years ago. What do you think is happening to that person on the inside? They are filled with hatred and anger and malice. They are never happy and walk around with a chip on their shoulder. I have learned most recently this life lesson: pray for them and let them have their space. For some, it might take longer than others, but they will come around in due time. God will work on them on their hearts. I have found a life filled with blessings on top of blessings when I am okay with those around me. My friendships are good; my family is good with me. I mention family because, yes, family can have conflict with us more than any other relationships we may have with others. I have known family members not speaking with one another for years. I have known children, adult children, not talking to parents. This really disturbs me. I would give anything to talk with my parents who are both deceased for many years now.

You choose what you want out of life. Are you going to be bitter or better from circumstances and situations? Do you want a life filled with blessings or curses? Again, the choice is yours to think about. Life is too short, and we have seen that during the past year with the pandemic. We see daily how precious life is, and how we respond to life is so vital to our happiness and successes in life here and beyond the days to come. Think about it, your future, our future, depends on how we respond to things today. Today might be that day that you send that text message, make that call, send that note via mail. (Yes, some people still mail cards and letters!) I love receiving them! I want to be better and not bitter. I want to grow and flourish as an individual, and that should be your desire as well, I know it is. Your desire to want to be a better person is what has you reading this book in the first place. Together we are both going to be better and greater than before!

Like mentioned before in this book, everything starts with the person in the mirror. It all starts with you and I. We must be the change, we must make the choice, and we must look at the outcome this will make in our lives if we choose to take the high road in circumstances that would normally leave us bitter. This has nothing to do with being weak, this has all to do with being the bigger and stronger person. Life is so full of situations where we can feel like we have been wronged, times when we feel like someone has gotten the best of us. Those are times when we can easily become bitter with the outcome. Life is not fair! We have heard that saying as long as we can remember. Life is not fair. No matter how many times we have heard that saying, it does not take the place for how we are feeling at the time. The feeling of disappointment and betrayal still hurts; and we, as mere humans, want our revenge. It's okay to feel this way. We all have felt this way at some time or another in life. Life is complicated, with circumstances and situations that make it even more complicated. I read somewhere once that only the people who say they love me are the only people who have hurt me. I have never been hurt by the enemy! I have not ever been hurt by a stranger or someone who knows me, only those who love me. This is a life lesson learned. I am learning all the time, every day, that people will hurt you and not think anything of it. No shame, no regrets. People are so cold. They will lie to you in your face and not even phase them. This is the society we are living in today. In my opinion, there is no loyalty anymore. Everyone is out for themselves. I believe in my heart that people were much nicer to one another when I was growing up. I really think that people cared for each other more than what we see today. We live in a society that has everyone looking out for one person and one person only, themselves. Life can be so hard and cruel. We have so many obstacles to conquer, and it can be tough to overcome them, but no one ever said life would be easy. Life simply is not fair. Nothing is fair about living in a world filled with hate and unkindness. It is easy to become bitter at things we see daily. I want to grow as a person. I want to be better than the day before. I want that for you as well.

Growing comes from letting go. Letting go is required in becoming better and not bitter in life. I have had situations in my life where becoming bitter was certainly easier than letting go, disappointments that caused me to even hate some people responsible for those disappointments. Life is full of lessons. Teaching moments are before us every single day. How we choose to respond? How will I react in those situations? Will you become bitter or better? This becomes an area in your life where you learn a lot about yourself. Learn to let go! My personal life has been filled with disappointments and setbacks, plenty of reasons to have bitterness. I can honestly say that there have been times I felt bitter, but not for long. I truly believe that blessings are tied to how we feel in our hearts and what we carry in our hearts. Knowing that alone, I have no place for bitterness in my heart. I have known people to hold grudges for years over things that no longer exist, haven't existed for years! This is wasted time. Time is too valuable to waste with bitterness in your heart. Holding on to grudges is not good for the person who harbors them in their heart. Yes, life is not fair. People let us down, people will disappoint us, but life goes on. Things will eventually work themselves out. Life has a way of doing that. Again, we must learn to trust the process. I have learned that in my almost sixty years of being here. Family are the one that will hold the greatest bitterness toward us. I can honestly say that in my personal life, many of my family members have not accepted the fact that I am a published author.

For whatever reason, I have so many family members who have yet once reach out to me to congratulate me about my accomplishments. This saddens me. I have friends as well that have yet to say great job to me. This hurts me also. I did not change; they did. I am still the same person that came from the cotton fields. People are funny, Daddy would always say to me as a child. People will let you down when you need them the most. Let your circle be small, Daddy would also tell me. I am seeing this more each day. I am where God placed me to be. Every day my life belongs to him. If I am successful or struggling, it's for his glory. Bitterness will never get you a blessed life. It will never take you to the level of greatness! On the other hand, if you are humble and stay on the path of lifting others up, this will certainly take you to places you would not have even imagined! I make it a point to cheer others on. For me, it's not a competition. I want all of us to win! Especially the people in my circle, my family and friends who are close to me. When they win, I feel like we all win! The only person I am in competition with is myself! Every day I want to be better than I was the day before. The pathway to greatness requires me to become better at myself. All that I need is to be better at becoming *me*! My mind is focused at becoming the best that I can be. No room for bitterness, no room for hatred. Trust me when I say, God has enough resources to bless us all! There is no lacking or shortage when it comes to being blessed by the creator of the universe. There is no need to hold bitterness in our hearts and expect to receive blessings. It just doesn't work that way.

Remember, when you forgive, you heal.
And when you let go, you grow.

Life lesson from this chapter:

My goal each day is to be better not bitter. I will not hold bitterness in my heart. I will learn to forgive and move on to greatness!

No God, No Peace!

Know God, Know Peace!

If I have learned one thing about living during this pandemic, it is the importance of a relationship with God. I can see it every day in my personal life. I have discovered that peace with God is all that matters at the end of the day. I made up my mind in the beginning of 2021 that I needed to personally return to my first love. That would be my relationship with God. I can say with no doubt that he has not always been the center of my life the past five years. I am writing this chapter, which is personal to me, but my hope that it is helpful to someone else out there that might be reading this right now. You are at the crossroad of your life right now. You need direction for the next step you will take. Do not take another step without God. You and I are here where we are right now because God has brought us this far. We have made it through every single day to be here. I have endured so much just to be right here in this moment called now! As I look back and see where I have come from, I realize that I have had nothing to do with it. God knows it was not my faithfulness, certainly wasn't my loyalty to him. I have discovered in the past year that true peace only comes from God and how we spend time with him.

Let me share with you the Johnny Martinez-Carroll that most people know or think that they know. I have come to know God the hard way. I was young and out of work years ago when I was working as an electrician at a local electrical contractor. I can assure you that God is working on your behalf even when you don't even know it or know him for that matter. God is so in touch with who you are without you even knowing he exist. I can personally share with you how he took care of me and looked out for me while I was just trying to figure him out! Talk about doors opening for me and placing the right people in your path. God will do that. He has done that for me so many times repeatedly. Like that time I had just gotten laid off from my job and walking out to my car as I was going to the unemployment office and a guy, Mike, called out to me and asked if I wanted to work in the warehouse starting the next day. One minute you're thinking how I am going to provide for my family, and God steps right in and provides you with a job when one job closes. He provides you with another one; he works like that. Some people say that he works in mysterious ways. We have all said that at one time or another. He already knows what you stand in need of, think about it. He already knows! That same year, a few months later, I was working in the warehouse one morning, getting an order ready for a truck before it left for the field. The company owner was addressing the crew about changes that were being made. I wasn't paying much attention as I was busy at the time when someone asked who warehouse foreman would be. He then calls my name.

He says to the group, "Johnny will be our new warehouse foreman as of today!"

God will promote you when you least expect it! I have learned in my life that your work ethic will open and close doors for you. When you think that no one is watching, rest assured that God is always looking out for you. He sees you and knows your heart. When it is time for elevation, he will put you in place. I can remember my daddy always saying that you want to be always on your best behavior at work, you never know who is watching. Daddy was always right. But it is not just work. Anytime and anywhere, you never know who is watching. God is always watching. He knows all. I recall having a conversation with the owner of that company that I worked for.

I asked Mr. Harville one day, "Why did you promote me that day?" He told me that he felt anywhere that he put me, I would do a great job! Our work ethic follows us. Who we are and what kind of person we are will follow us in life. Again, it will open or close doors for you. The peace of God is so beautiful. He wants to live in you and me. He wants what is best for you and me.

I write about how he has been so good to me, but I want to share of some not-so-good times too. Like the time when I got laid off again later, and this time there was no job waiting before I got to my car. I was with no job for almost two years. Looking for work and interviewing, only to be disappointed time after time, driving around in an old beat-up truck with bad tires. One day I recall having two flat tires in the same day! Or that day when I drove to Brenham, Texas, for a job interview and got two traffic tickets the same day! I was thinking, *I really need to get this job now just to pay for these tickets!* People may look at my life and see the glory without knowing my story! When you see Johnny Martinez-Carroll, you see the college graduate without seeing the struggle and the late nights staying up writing school papers and turning in assignments. You might even look at my life as a licensed electrician, but what you fail to see was that young electrician that was starting out learning a trade that he really did not want to learn. But my dad talked me into learning a trade that would change my life forever. Thirty-eight years later I am still doing electrical work. You might even look at my life and see Johnny Martinez-Carroll, the published author, but even that came by just writing about my life stories growing up, having a close friend talk me into putting those stories in a book, *The Silent Dreamer*. I have endured hardships in life that I have mentioned in my writings, some have yet to be written about, but through it all, God has been a constant source of comfort and blessing to me. I can honestly say that life with Jesus is much better. Trust me, I have tried without him and have endured the chaos that goes with not knowing of his peace. God is about love and peace. He is not a God of confusion. If you are confused today, chances are that he is not in the center of your life. He is not in the center of your decisions and the choices you are making. There is nothing confusing about God. Read that again. I can also mention that each time God has not been in my decision-making, I have failed each time. Even when I thought I was winning, I was failing, and the results of those choices would eventually show up in other areas of my life. No God, no peace! This pretty much explains itself. When you know him and he is amid all you do, your life is going to be so much blessed. I am not saying everything is going to be blue skies and green fields all the time, but you will be able to handle what comes your way because of who has your back. God has promised to never leave you, nor forsake you. He is a friend who sticks closer than any brother. The year of this pandemic has taught us the importance of having a relationship with God, who loves us so much and wants to be first in our lives. I am learning each day that when he isn't first, I am at my worst! It's that plain and simple. When you know God, you know peace!

He wants you and me to experience the abundant life, a life that is filled with blessings on top of blessings. I have seen God work in my personal life so many times, especially in the not-so-good times and in times when I did not deserve his goodness because of my sins. I am so glad that because of his mercies, we are not consumed! A step to becoming better at who we are is accepting that we need a savior in our lives. We need Jesus. I need him in all that I put effort in. It does not matter if it's in my job daily or when I am volunteering in the community; I need his presence to show up and that he is seen in my character.

My grandson recently celebrated his fourteenth birthday. Jaiden is growing up so fast. Seems like yesterday he was just a baby. I tell him almost every time we talk, just be respectful to everyone, always show respect. That is how I want to live my life: always show Jesus. The world really needs it currently. In wanting to become greater, we must realize that we need Jesus in every situation and circumstance. Peace comes when we know him. The pathway to becoming greater will lead you to knowing God in his fullness. He made us for greatness! We were made for greater purpose in life. We were not made to just exist. We are walking greatness in his image! Learn to live in greatness.

The fear of the Lord is the beginning of wisdom: and knowledge of the holy is understanding. (Prov. 9:10 KJV)

God is so in love with you and me. We cannot even imagine what he wants to do in our lives and how much he wants to pour out his blessings. I will be the first to tell you that not everyone will understand when you desire to live and give your life to Christ. The true meaning of life comes when we totally surrender to him. When we make up our minds to become greater, it begins with the one who gave us the abundant life to live. The one and only who can give us the true meaning of peace, his perfect peace. Life during a pandemic has taught us that we need his mercy and grace through these uncertain times. We need comfort, answers. We need assurance that everything will be all right. We need Jesus! He is the only answer for the uncertainty of today. We are living in times where from one day to another we don't know what is going to happen next, but we do know who brings tomorrow. Somewhere I read that nothing last forever, not even our troubles. But I can say that God does last forever and he never changes. He will always be loving, caring, forgiving, and full of mercy forever. His love endures forever. This chapter is something that I loved writing. I wanted this to be for last; but I could not resist sharing this good news with you, this news of love, hope, faith and mercy that is beyond what you and I could ever imagine. My personal relationship with God has been a bumpy ride for the most part, a roller coaster of events has happened since my last book, *The Silent Dreamer*. Since the release of that book, I have changed jobs. I am now working for another local nonprofit in the area, Methodist Children's Home Family Outreach. My role with this organization is case manager. Changing jobs in the middle of a pandemic was a challenge, but here I am, being the happiest I have been in a while. My role here is part of a ministry with the organization. I get to help families that are in a hard place, families that need hope. I get to see daily the effects of how a community that comes together can make a difference in the life of a family in need. I share this with you because at the end of the day, I want to be the hands and feet of Jesus! I want to be the reason people see and come to know Jesus. That is all that matters when all is said and done. What I like about MCH Family Outreach is that it has great leadership, strong leaders. In my short time there, I have noticed this already, something my last job was lacking in.

Methodist Children's Home Family Outreach is a ministry with people who love the Lord. I needed that in my life. God knew what I needed, and he placed me here. I love how God places you and the right people you need in your life at the right time. His timing is always perfect. I recently had a conversation with a close friend. I shared with him the importance of looking over our own lives and taking inventory of how good God has been to us, even in our sins. If he can bless us in our sinful living, can you image what he has in store for us when we decide to live for him with all our being? I have mentioned before, and I will say it again, in all this uncertainty, God remains as the only one we can rely on and depend on. He never changes; he will never change! Even in my sinful nature, his love for me never changes. He loves you, and I the same, regardless of what we have done or will do. Know God, know peace like you've never known before. The Bible calls it perfect peace! I know all about chaos, all about hurt and disappointment, been there and done that many times over. But I also know the flip side of that pain and disappointment, a loving God who can take that pain away and restore you. Return to your first love and experience the abundant life he wants you to have. His love for you will never fail. This love is everlasting! Unlike any other kind of love you and I will ever experience! You will also experience how God intended for you and I to become great! We have greatness within us! To know God is to know His greatness and his great plan for us!

Friends, this chapter is basically my personal testimony, receiving His mercy and grace at the lowest point of my life, being jobless and feeling hopeless at the same time. Someone reading this might be in this situation this very moment. If you aren't in a relationship with God this very moment, let me recommend to Jesus! If you do know him and are in this situation right now of being jobless and hopeless, continue to seek him faithfully. He hasn't forgotten about you!

Life lesson from this chapter:

God loves you no matter where you are currently in life! Seek him, he is waiting for you!

Your Past Is Not Your Future!

Thank God the title of this chapter is true! Your past is not your future! So grateful here. My past is filled with pain and things I would rather not think about much continue to live in. Growing up in poverty, my life is so filled with riches, like a family who loves me and cares for me and friends who have stood by me through the good and bad. I can honestly say that I am rich! I am sure if you look back on where you've come from, you are rich too! Our past is just that, the past. Leave it there. People, including myself, relive the past. Those demons have a habit of rising up and take us to a place of fear and doubt. We all have demons we wrestle with. My past is different from your past, but we all have this one thing in common: we all have a past.

Let me take you on a journey of my past. I grew up in poverty, on a cotton plantation. My life was filled with people that played an important role in childhood. You can say they helped shape and mold me. I am sure you had some people as well that, looking back, you can say the same thing about. I have many from my past that are no longer here today, saints and soldiers who have since gone to live in glory with Jesus. Growing up in cotton fields on hot sunny days are a part of my past. I knew at an early age, this would be no part of my future. My past would also include living in shack of a wood-frame house with no running water, cold in the winter and hot in the summertime. My past was filled with dirt roads and a lot of walking. My past was in no way easy. Yours may be just as hard with similar or different obstacles, but here we are today. We have survived our past. We have come this far in life. God knows I could have given up many times, and many times I wanted to. Life is filled with circumstances and is complicated enough, but when you throw in poverty and not much to look forward to in life, this is all a recipe for failure. I must be honest here, I never really imagined myself living a better life than the one I was dealt living on that farm, as much as I wanted a better life. I have learned with time, especially this past year with all of its craziness, to trust the process, trust the author of your life. God himself will see you through. My past is filled with both great times and not-so-great times. Looking back, I can see that I am living my purpose, as we speak. Like the old saying goes, your rear-view mirror is smaller than your windshield. Everything you left behind is smaller than what is in front of you! You have so much in front to look forward to. You have your dreams and goals in front of you, things you want to accomplish that are just waiting on you. My past is filled with lots of disappointments, closed doors in my face, things I felt were meant for me but just did not work out in my favor. Trust me, growing up where I grew up, I never saw being a college graduate, published author, and having a job where I am doing what I always wanted to do: helping others. This was not in my plans at all as a kid. To be honest, as a young adult, I never saw any of this in my future. I have said it before, I will say it again—trust the process and trust the One who is in control of the process.

You can't have a positive life with a negative mind. (Unknown)

In order to move ahead, the past must be left behind. It's not a part of who you were meant to be in your future. You were made and meant for great things. This book was written with that concept in mind. You are greater than you think. You are braver than you thought you were. You are stronger than you imagined. We are resilient when we are forced to be. When our backs are to the wall, we have within us what it takes to come out fighting. Our past however keeps us from fighting many times. Our past sometimes has a way of following us into our future. I know that from my own life.

I know that because of my past experiences with trusting people, I don't always trust others easily. The pain of being hurt and broken has scarred me. If I trust you, you have made a huge gain by having my trust in you. I don't issue that out very easily. I know that this is about my past hurts and disappointments, but I am working on this and getting better with time.

Move forward from your past. Easily said than done, but necessary in life, necessary for your mental state of mind. Moving on is not always easy. To be honest, most of the time it's difficult to adjust to things about our past in order to move on. I have many times tried to move on from a bad experience and find myself living in my past or focusing on something that has happened and would not let me move forward. Again, I want to focus on my word for the year: *resilient*, the ability to recover quickly from a difficult circumstance, toughness. This is required in order to move forward from our past. We must become resilient. I chose this word at the beginning of 2021. Resilience is what my life reflects, summed up in a nutshell. Having to bounce back from all the obstacles I have endured in my life past and present, looking back growing up in extreme poverty—this was preparing me for things ahead. We talked about closed doors and missed opportunities. These things will happen in life. They have in mine, and I am sure you have experienced them too. But when all is said and done, I want to be able to say that I am a better person because of my past. My past has made me the man that I am today. This is a daily process. Each day we work at this. You come to the conclusion that you are becoming greater as a person because of your past. My past is helping me to build character. My past is allowing me to see the good in others. I am so glad that I am not defined by the mistakes I have made in my life. Some I have not learned to let go yet; others I have clearly moved on from. Living in your past limits your future. Let's read that last sentence again. Living in your past limits your future! This, my friend, is a stumbling block for future blessings, future winnings, a future that is filled with God's best for you and favor. Trust me when I say that your past does not have to define your future. I am living proof. Thank God for that. You were made for greatness, regardless of your past and the mistakes that you and I have made. We were made to be great! Tell yourself this affirmation each day: "I was made for greatness. I was made in the image of the highest God."

I Am Not a Failure!

It does not matter how many mistakes you have made, past or present. You are not a failure! I have thought many times in my adulthood life that I was failing, that I had failed in life. I am sure we all feel this way at times, that we look back and count the times we have failed at something. I can recall a time when I had a small gift-shop in the small community I grew up in Snook, Texas. Most people probably do not even remember this small shop, Lighthouse Gifts. It was a small store that years earlier was a café in Snook. My daughter, wife, and I operated it. We sold things like home décor, candles, and various items. I was excited about the opportunity of having my own business. It was open for about ten to eleven months. I would love to tell you that it was a success, but it was not at all. My dreams of being a business owner was short lived. I wasn't even making enough to cover the utility bills. I recall some Saturdays sitting there alone without any customers visiting that day and sitting there in tears because my dreams were so big and my hopes were just as big! The quiet boy from the farm wanted something big that people would enjoy, that boy dreamed more than he planned. I have always been this way. My mind has opened to failures as lessons. I have learned from them. The goals and dreams are still there, but I have refocused and reloaded. I can look back and see that those failures were a part of the process. I find myself in a good place today. My expectations and dreams are still big, but I also know that if they don't work out, it's okay too. Go at it from a different approach next time. Key words in that last sentence: *next time*. And there will be next times. There will always be more opportunities. You will always have more dreams. If you are like me, you are not done dreaming yet! You have not failed; you just got started on the road to success!

Some people have been handed down their successes. They have inherited their money, the company. They are where they are because of someone else's hard work. Then you have those who have sweated, worked hard, and even cried in the middle of a store with no customers! I am not even close where I want to be, but I am on the right path. So are you. Our past is just stepping-stones to get to where we want to be in life. Our past is not our future. Continue the course. Stay in your lane. Stand in your circle. Let no one knock you off. Fight, crawl if you must, but never let anyone have your square. Stay on the course. Becoming great is all about bouncing back from past failures and setbacks. You and I were made for this moment in life. This is our time. This is your moment of greatness. It is your time to shine. Leave your past behind!

You cannot change what you did before,
But you can change what you do next.

We have heard so many times, "Thank God I am not what I used to be." I can speak from both my history and experience in life that I am thankful for that. I have more work to do in order to become better than I was. I realize that you and I may be on the same path to discovering our better selves. Keep moving forward; keep pushing daily. All I want is to be better today than I was yesterday. This should be our goal and plan as human beings in this world filled with hatred. Move forward. Proceed with your plans. Forgive yourself. Your past is not your future. This is your new season. Embrace it. You are about to step into some exciting times. You will be the best at what you do! Thank God that my pathway to greatness is not tied to my past! I am so glad that in all of my mistakes in life, I am still destined to become the person God intended me to become, regardless of my ugly past. Someone reading this right now is thinking the same thing. My friend, your past is not your future. You are becoming greater as we speak. We were made for this moment of greatness, regardless of our past. This is exciting news. Maybe the best news you will hear today will be that you are greater than you think!

Life lesson from this chapter:

My past does not define my future! Everything that is in front of me is good. My better days are in front of me!

Choose Your Words!

We become what we believe. We also become what we speak. What words are you using? *I can* and *I will* are words we can use to encourage ourselves. Think about the words you use to describe yourself. I have known people who never use positive words or they never use words of affirmation. These same people will never get well, never get out of debt. They will never live their dreams. The same people will never experience any more than the average, simply because of the words they choose to speak! Think about it, words like "I will never" or "I can't." Here are some others: "That is not meant for me" and "I am not good enough or smart enough." These words will never take you far. I have spoken these for a good part of my life. I have lived in these words and have not succeeded at all. These words bring on defeat not success. You not only bring about what you think about, but the same applies to the words you speak about yourself. Change your vocabulary and you change your life!

For the first time in my adult life, I truly feel that I can accomplish anything that I set out to do! I know that I will give it a try before I would ever say that I can't do something. A person only fails after he has tried, and even then, it's a lesson learned on how to try again from another approach. Try again after making the necessary changes! Choose words that uplift and encourage, words that pull you up, not tear you down. Whether you realize it or not or you accept it or not, you were made to influence.

I can recall my children growing up. I can remember saying to them all the time, "You can do anything you set out to do!" It is so vital to the mindset of our children to hear words of encouragement daily, that as a young child they hear that they can achieve anything in life, words that make them believe in themselves. Parents, this is so vital to their success in life. As much as I know, my dad loved me by the things he did for me. He never said many words like this to me, although he did influence me to learn a trade. Again, we are talking about being an influence. He talked me into believing that I could learn a trade. Almost forty years later, I am still doing electrical work. People that influence use words that encourage. Think about it, all the motivational speakers, life coaches, leadership coaches, and others who influence people use the same language. They use the same words, words that lift up and encourage. What kind of coach would I be if I used words that did not build you up? I love my current job. Besides helping people with needs, I get to encourage them daily by speaking words that helps lift them up, words that give them hope. At the end of the day, don't we all want that anyway? We all want hope for a better future, a better tomorrow. We all want hope for a better right now moment! In order to have this hope, we need to learn to speak words that will take us there.

Change your words, and you change your life.

Instead of saying words like, "I cannot do that, I don't know how to do that," learn to say words like, "I cannot do that, but I am willing to learn how to do that. I am open to learning new things." We can learn to do amazing things in life if only we change how we speak and if we are open to learning new things in life. I am learning each day as I grow older the importance of speaking words that make us think of where we want to be in life. We all want to succeed and do great things that will leave a legacy behind. Unfortunately, growing up, I never heard many words that made me feel like I could achieve much. I do have some stories where people in my life inspired me to keep going, to keep dreaming. The right words spoken into your life will keep you going. They will keep you dreaming! My GED teacher, Mrs. Dorothy Crowson comes to mind. She told me that I had what it took to continue my education. She believed in me. Her words made me think about how far could I really go with my education after receiving my GED. It took me twenty years, but eventually, I enrolled taking college courses online with the University of Phoenix. When people believe in you, they speak the right words to encourage you. I have learned, when the right words are spoken, you are limitless in your possibilities. You become unstoppable!

When my kids were growing up, I would leave for work early long before they would get up for their school day. I made it a habit to leave them behind handwritten notes to encourage them for the day. I have also done the same with my grandson Jaiden. To this day in our hallway bathroom taped on the vanity mirror are notes that I have left for him. For example, "Jaiden, you have all the tools to become great, love Papa." Here is another one: "Jaiden, always believe in yourself, love Papa." I often think what turns my life would have taken if I had those kinds of words spoken to me as a child? Words are funny. They are not forgotten, the good and the bad. Words hurt and sting for a lifetime. You remember the compliments just like you do the words that made us feel hurt. If someone says to you, "I don't love you anymore," you eventually forget the person. They fade and become a memory, a good one or a bad one, but their words remain forever.

My sweet mother went to live with the Lord in December of 1997. I still remember one of our last conversations we had before she died. What words will you leave behind to your loved ones? What will they have to remember you by? Choose your words wisely. Those words spoken here on earth will last into eternity. Start today by speaking words of encouragement, words to inspire those around you. Words that lift up can change a person's attitude about life. It can make them believe in themselves like never before. Positive words can be a game changer in someone's life. It can be the push or nudge that they might be needing to get to the next level. Words are powerful. They either hurt or help. Words are also not forgotten easily. The sting of hurtful words can last a lifetime. I have had compliments that I received years ago about my work ethic or just about who I am as a person and still recall those kind words spoken to me. I also have had the opposite harsh words, which I have never gotten over. Words can either make your day or break your day. They can make you feel so great, spoken to encourage, or they can keep you down in the dumps. Choose your words wisely. What kind of words will you speak into others? How will your words impact and influence others?

Be careful with your words,
they can only be forgiven not forgotten.

I love sharing my life story with others. I truly feel that my words can influence others to work hard in life. I feel that my words can help change someone's mind about getting an education at an early age and going further in life because of it. Words that inspire and cause change in a person's life and behavior, change in the way that they think about themselves. Words that are spoken with that effect will change the world that we live in. I was recently talking about this with a team member at work, how today we are bombarded with so much hate and so much hate-filled words in the news. I filled in my opinion. We are at the darkest place I have ever seen this world in my fifty-nine years of living. Hate words fill our news daily, social media outlets, almost every story has words that pull people down and no uplifting whatsoever. When our words change, our thinking will change also. The words that we hear will stay with us forever. The card will get misplaced, the gift will either break or get lost. It happens! But the words that we hear from a person who loves us will forever remain in our hearts. As I write this book, my daughter whom I have mentioned earlier is currently writing her first book. I would like to think that my story has inspired her to write a book about her life stories as a young single mom raising a boy at that time. This will inspire and help other single moms to push through and keep fighting. Even when it does not look like you are going to win, you can win! I am so proud of her and of the woman she has become, with one master's degree already and soon to have another. Choosing your words, again, will change your life. I cannot stress this enough. Going from "I can't" to "I will," you don't even have to put a time limit on it, just do it! Words that are spoken to help and encourage keep away confusion and strife. Those kinds of words keep us from getting angry and remove any room for arguments and misunderstandings. They keep us at peace with one another.

A soft answer turneth away wrath: but grievous words stir up anger. (Prov. 15:1 KJV)

Looking back in my own life, I can see situations where my words could have been different and saved myself a lot of pain and heartache. My words could have prevented an argument and misunderstanding. Kinder words, words spoken in love. I am sure we all have felt this way before at some time or another. We speak quickly without even thinking. It happens. We have all spoken and regretted saying things that were hurtful. I know personally that I have many times, more times than I care to remember. The abovementioned verse says "a soft answer." We should think before we speak. We should think before we give someone a piece of our mind. As we often say, words hurt. They hurt more than we will admit. Words have such an impact on our lives, how we express them and how we receive them. They either make us feel good, or they don't. It's that simple. The same applies with the words that you use daily, the words that you use to speak about yourself. They either help or hurt. You either believe you can do something, or you don't. If you don't speak words of affirmation about yourself, you will not believe in yourself.

Speak daily words that lift up and encourage you and others. It is so vital to your self-confidence. If you have the right words spoken to you and if you believe in speaking these words to yourself daily, you can become unstoppable! Think of what you can achieve if you only believe in yourself. Change the words you speak about yourself and the words you speak into others! Words are so powerful, and when they are spoken to inspire and to lift up, they leave a lasting impact on the person receiving them. Change your words. Which would you rather say and believe, "I am never going to get out of debt" or "I am taking steps to get out of debt, one debt at a time"? The same with people who say these words: "I am never going to get well. I will always be sick." Instead, change your words and speak, "I am getting better each day. I feel better today than I felt yesterday."

This is the power of changing our words and changing our lives for the better, believing that we can accomplish and achieve more than ever before in our lives. This is your power! I refuse to speak words that are negative, words that put down and not lift up! Think about how some people only hear these types of words spoken into their lives. I was in the store recently. I heard a young mother call her young child. He must have been around five or six years old. She cursed at him, called him horrible names, trying to get his attention. I said to myself, "That kid has no future!" His future is filled with disappointment if that is what he is hearing now at a young age. Those words have a way of cutting at our spirit. Those words would make me feel useless and damage my self-esteem and self-worth. Trust me, words hurt! Hurtful words are not forgotten. Words spoken with hate and malice live forever. Words that hurt have a way of hurting for a long time, even a lifetime! In my work with counseling kids a few years ago, I can recall being told how some parents would say words to their kids that might not have been meant for hurt, but they did hurt in the end. Words are very powerful; speak them wisely. We seem to take for granted what we say to others and not realize the good or the damage we do when we speak to others. These same power in our words can be used to change a person's life for the best! Positive words spoken in love make such a great difference in the life of someone who is doing their best. If we speak words that will inspire, that person will live a life that has great possibilities, endless possibilities!

Power is in the tongue; it can build up and it can destroy! Looking back at my time with my GED teacher, Ms. Crowson, she spoke words to me that made me believe in myself. I find myself mentioning her in a lot in my writings. She spoke words that made me who I am today. That is how the power of words work. They inspire and influence us to work hard. They can be the difference in our lives to accomplish goals. Words can be that powerful! Words can help us discover our greatness! Make it a habit to speak words that lift up, words that reflect greatness. This is so powerful and much needed today. When I think about our youth today, they need words that will inspire them to want to change and want positive change in their lives. Our youth today need to hear words spoken to them regularly that will encourage them. Words can be that powerful and have much impact. As I have spoken before about my dad speaking to me. I can remember words he shared with me, and he has been gone almost thirty-eight years now. Words spoken with love and meant to encourage you will live forever. Listen to the words you are using each day. Pay attention to how you speak to your children, your spouse, your friends, and your coworkers. Pay attention to how you speak to yourself! I am constantly reminding myself to use words that lift me up as well. The words that I use should make me feel confident in my own skin also. At the end of the day, words are so powerful!

> **Speak life, speak love,**
> **Speak bravery and kindness and hope,**
> **Speak wisdom and truth.**

Life lesson from this chapter:

Speak words that inspire and influence others to do great things! Speak words of wisdom!

The "Role" Call

I have had the wonderful opportunity of meeting some amazing people in my lifetime. This is the part of my book where I want to pay tribute to them. I got the idea for listing names from the Bible. The book of Matthew records the genealogy of Jesus. The names are mentioned of how Jesus came to be. I wanted to do something similar with names of people who have influenced my life, people who have encouraged me in some way or another. Most of the people named in this chapter have passed away, some are still here, and some would be unmentioned because I just cannot name everyone. We are all called to influence others. We have the opportunity to make an impact on the lives of those we are in contact with daily. Writing this book has taken me places that I have not been there for some time. It has made me take long look at where I have been and the people who made it possible for me, or at least had a hand in helping me get there: my family, friends, coworkers, former teachers. Some are my electrical customers; some are people I had met once and never saw them again; some are people that I never met in person just on social media. But these are names of people that influenced me in some way over the years.

Some people will be the obvious, my parents, of course, and my GED teacher, Ms. Crowson; but others will be friends that I have made along the way through years of volunteering. Years of giving back has put me in the presence of so many great people that have inspired me to keep going. Words that were spoken to me from people who care about me, people who love me, and I know without a doubt that they did. Something that I have learned in this past year is that people can pop in and out of your life, but the ones who were meant to stay will stay. They will be loyal till the end. And even if they are not always around; they are just a phone call away from you. You will always be able to count on them no matter what. Some people will not always be there. Maybe for whatever reason, their part in your life is over. It's time to move forward without them. It's okay! They had a place once, but that part is over. It's time for something new; it's time for new people. That is the biggest lesson learned. There will always be new people in your life, always.

To be honest, we only have a few friends that stick around. Life happens, as we have often heard. But new ones will come in and go out too. That is life in a nutshell. People will sow into our lives, and so will we into the lives of those around us. I love having the opportunity to influence those around me. I absolutely love it. I know with no doubts whatsoever that my parents instilled in me the act of kindness, helping others when they are in need, for that I am grateful to them. I love them so much for teaching me this valuable lesson in life. Rest in peace.

Growing up on that farm I got to know two men who later in my life became like dads to me: Sammie Elmore and Willie B. Amos. These two men were a huge help when my dad passed away in 1984. Mr. Elmore was the first person to talk with me when I got the news of my dad. Mr. Amos and I were at the same church years later and both on the deacon board. He was like my second dad. He was a man that I truly looked up to. May both of these influencers in my life rest in peace.

There are many others to mention from Old Bethlehem Baptist Church that really influenced my life during my time there as a deacon and as a church member: Deacons Smith, Tilman, Blake and Lister. These men have all gone on to live with Jesus, but their influence on my life lives still. May you all rest in peace.

My aunt Santos was like a second mom to me. She was like a mother to me even when my mother was still here with me. She remained a mother to me after my mom passed and until she passed on herself. Thank you for treating me like a son always. I never knew a woman who worked harder than she did. Rest in peace.

I have volunteered with MDA summer camp in the past. Some of my best friends were made during those camp years. I have been so blessed to know these people and to have them in my life for many years: Dalia Deleon, Colleen Ernst, Curt Bendix, Katie Lowe, Alex Knoll, just to name a few. MDA camp taught me so much about working as a team. I carry those values with me even today in the workplace. We can get so much done when we work together as one, working for a common cause. This applies even today with those who are around at work. Teamwork really does make the dream work!

Thank you to Little Flock Baptist Church and the many people of the Wilcox community that helped to shape and mold me. Mr. and Mrs. Henry Wiley, these two people were like the grandparents that I never had. Thank you for your role in my life. May you rest in peace. Honey Rogers, Odessa Hinton, Ida Kemp, Alvin Walton— these people mentioned here are so vital to my growth as a young Christian.

In 1982, I went to work for a local electrical contractor. Harville Electric Company was at that time one of the biggest electrical companies in the Bryan College Station area. My cousin Roy was working there and got me set up for an interview. Here I am almost forty years later still in the electrical field. I am so thankful to Robert (Bob) Harville for giving me the opportunity to learn a trade that I still use today.

Thank you to Mike Estes who called me as I was walking to my car that day I was laid off when work was slow. Mike gave me a job on the day I was sent home. That warehouse job led to a promotion later as warehouse foreman. Thank you, Mike, for believing in me. Thanks to my dad for pushing me to learn a trade that would make me a living wage for most of my adult life. I have mentioned so many times how my father told me years ago: if I learned a trade, I would always have a job! As always, Daddy was correct! I worked with many people while at this electric company. One of my biggest influencers was an old guy named Sylvester K. We knew him as simply CO. He really made an impact on me. He had so many years of experience over a young electrician like myself at the time. Thanks for believing in me and teaching me. Rest in peace, CO.

What I love about small town living is that so many people are involved in your growing up and you get to know them personally: family friends, people who you can look back and recall something special they have done for you, done for your family, your loved ones. This is a good time to look back and reflect on some people who have influenced you in your life. Think of those who have helped you along the way. If you are like me, there are too many to name, but the fact remains there is a roll call of influencers, a list of people who have believed in you when some did not.

When I was in school, maybe seventh grade, Mr. Richard Kovar was my favorite teacher. He taught me Texas history. To this day he is best storyteller ever! I really loved being in his class and listening to him share stories with the class. Thank you, Mr. Kovar, for being an influence in my life. Rest in peace.

My cousin Roy, this guy taught me almost all that I know about electricity. He was my first mentor in this field of work. Roy is not only my cousin, but he is my brother also. We both grew up together, and sometimes we were both literally in the same home. Roy and my mother were first cousins, the kids of two siblings. I love Roy with all my heart. He was my big brother growing up. No was one was going to bother me if he was around. He would fight a bear for me in a heartbeat! I could literally write an entire chapter on my cousin Roy. He means that much to me, but for now I will simply say, thank you, Roy, for always having my back and for always being my cousin, my friend, my mentor, and, most of all, my brother. I love you till the end. I feel like everyone has a cousin who is more like a brother or a sister to them. You are that close. Roy is that person in my life. Even though our lives have taken different paths since our days as kids, we need to talk more and laugh at old times more!

Dan Kiniry is another person in my life who has influenced me to make this world a better place to live in. I can start in my local community to make it better. Dan is responsible for Community Potluck, a group that meet each Sunday at a local park pavilion to share a meal and conversation with the homeless and less fortunate. This group has met for thirteen years now, rain or shine, holiday. This weekly event goes on. I love attending and talking to people whom I consider my friends. Dan is also responsible for Tiny Hope Village, a community for small homes for people who are homeless. This project is still in progress, but I can assure you, with land already purchased, it will have homes on it soon. Thanks for influencing me to do my part, my brother.

My family is the greatest source of influence in my life. My sisters, whom I love them all. It's so funny how all my life I have been around women, the only boy to so many sisters. Even at work, I am around women who have influenced me in so many ways. My sisters are so important to me, and they are my support system, my rock. I know they will be there for me without a doubt. They always have. My sisters Margaret and Mary have been with me since our days growing up on that farm with literally nothing. They have been with me from day one. We all struggled together with very little in terms of material things. We always knew our mother did her best for us. We always felt her love. I do not get to see them as often as I would like, but here is where I want to say thank you to them both for always believing in their brother and most of all for loving me.

People come in and out of our lives. Some inspire us to be the best we can be while others cause us to stress! Choose your circle wisely. Thank God for the people who have spoken words to me over the course of my life that spoke life into me! I think that I have shared the story about the car salesman interview years ago. I was looking for work and at that time very desperate for any job. I applied for a job at a car dealership. This was years ago, and my selection of clothes was very limited, but I put on my best that day. I was young and had been out of work for some time. My best pair of jeans and button-down shirt was not impressive for the interviewer. His first words to me were, "You will never sell cars dressed like that." That left a lasting impression on me! I was hurt for two reasons: I really needed a job and I was wearing the best that I had at that time. To this very day I believe in dressing up for the part. While some might believe that I overdress, I do not think that at all. I have been in the professional work setting for five years now, and I dress the part every day! I cannot remember the name of the guy who interviewed me at that car lot, but he taught me a lot about myself the day that he denied me that job selling cars for him. I guess you can say that he influenced me!

I certainly believe that inspiration comes in many forms. It can be wrapped up in different paper! I have many friends that I have made through social media, people that I have never met personally and probably never will, but they have inspired me nonetheless. Some are friends and former students from my days with the University Phoenix as an online student. Thank God for my education as it has opened doors for me. Leigh Paugh is a friend I made while a student at UOP. She was a team member of mine, so we got to know each other well working on team assignments together. Leigh loves the Lord, and I love Leigh! Thank you so much for inspiring me in both school and my personal growth as a Christian. Crissy Leigh Featherstone is another student from UOP that has been a constant friend and supporter. She has inspired me in so many ways during my school days and just with life in general. Thank you for always being in my corner.

I lost my sister Katie Ruth while writing this chapter of my book. May you rest in peace. I am so glad we got a chance to meet in person over three years ago. You will forever be in my thoughts, my dear sister. When I received word that Kate had passed, my first reaction was sadness, but then I really did not know how to feel. I realized as days went by that this woman, who I only got to know for a short time, was my sister, my dad's daughter. That made me feel sadness and hurt. I have learned through all of this that people come into your life for a reason and some for a season. It was meant for Kate and I to meet. The time we had together was short, but we always will have an attachment, our dad. She has inspired me to love my family even more, spend time with those who love and care about me even more. Time with them is precious. Our loved ones are here one day, and they are gone the next.

We have people in our lives we need to apologize to, phone calls that need to be made. We need to get busy fixing things with the people that we love. With all that is going on in the world today, it's not even about what happens next week or next month. Each day we have is so precious. Life is precious. The people who are mentioned in this chapter are precious to me. They have encouraged and influenced me in some way. All of them have a place not only in my life, but also in my heart forever.

My friend Barbara Knowles is another friend of mine from the Community Potluck group. She is faithful to this group especially those who attend and just need prayer or just a listening ear. Barbara is also a published author herself. She has inspired me to continue to write and share my story with others. I have learned that people who influence come from all walks of life, encouragement can come from anyone in many forms. Barbara loves the Lord, and she loves his children, all of them, especially the homeless and the ones in jail. I started writing inmates on death row because of Barbara and her communication with those behind bars. Community Potluck is a huge influence in my life. The group itself is important to me. This group has taught me so much about compassion and empathy. It has taught me about loving people who need love the most. I have mentioned this group before. The impact it has on me is priceless.

Becoming great involves being influenced by great people! I have had my share of these people in my life. Both men and women who taught me valuable lessons about life in general. It takes a village, we have heard so many times. It takes so many people to help and influence those around us. The more that I write, the more that I think of those people in my life both now and then as a young poor kid growing up on that farm. I am not sure what people thought of this kid back then. Did they see me as someone who was going to make something of himself? Probably not. Even I couldn't see that back then. All that I could see was how I could leave the farm. There were times that I could not even see that. My options were limited back then, but those who influenced me were all around me from an early age, from Mr. Willie Williams and his wife, Miss Rosie, to my aunt Hannah Carroll.

The road to greatness is paved by those who have gone before us and who have influenced us along the way. I recently paid a visit to my home church, Old Bethlehem Church, on the Sunday that I was there. I noticed the empty pews. Gone were the old saints who were there years ago when I was a member there. It is so sad to look over and not see some of the familiar faces of years ago. Time goes on; life goes on. The land stays the same in the same location, but the owners change! This is a quote that I remember hearing Deacon Smith say all the time. This man of great wisdom was over 100 years old when he passed on. He was either 102 or 103 years old. I recall sitting with him in our deacon meetings. He would always say that he wanted to hear from the "young deacon." He wanted to hear his opinion. That young deacon would be me! The youngest in the room. Sitting among those great men, I was in the middle of greatness! Greatness was all around me each time we gathered.

Looking back, the people named in this chapter all played a part in my life. The pathway to greatness is traveled by those who have come before you. I want more than anything to leave a legacy for my children and grandchildren. I want to play a role in their lives, just like the people mentioned in this chapter. I want them to experience greatness at the highest level. I want them to know that they were made for this moment of being great. I could only hope that when I am long gone, they would have memories of how I lived and how I wanted my life to inspire them to be their very best. As parents and grandparents, isn't that what we all want out of life? I truly believe that my mom and dad would both be so proud of me today, not because I have published a book but because of the man they shaped me to be. When my time here on earth is done, I hope that my name will be remembered on someone's role call list too! My kids and family inspire me. They influence me to be the best that I can be. They inspire me to greatness!

To this day, my greatest influence was my dad. Let me just say that he never spoke a bad word to me. Never in his lifetime did he use profanity in front of me, as a child or a man. He only spoke words that encouraged me, very mild mannered. My dad talked to me daily and shared with me what I needed to know to be great even as a young child. He always wanted better for me. I can name many people, but none will compare to my dad. I wanted to be like him in raising my own children. I believe I did my best impression of him with my kids. I wanted to always speak words that lift them up. I never once ever talked to them with harsh words. I never wanted to speak to them and have their spirits broken. As parents we have such a huge role to play in the future of our kids. Just by the words we use around them will shape them or break them later in life. Fathers, please be very cautious of how you speak to your sons and daughters. You're the spiritual leader of your home. Be sure your words are kind and refreshing to those in your house. Be kind to your wife. Speak sweet words to her always. Be the influence and impact of your home! Think about this. The way you impact those around you will lead you to greatness! The book of Proverbs teaches us that "a good name is to be chosen rather than great riches."

That name will elevate you toward greatness! Think of the people in your life that have influenced you, made an impact in your life. If you cannot name any, maybe you need to make new friends! I have met so many wonderful people since my first book was published, people who have also written a book and have made an impact in my life in meeting this past year. Each book event that I have attended has put me in position to meet some awesome people. These people have influenced me so much. We support each other on social media. We talk on the phone and encourage each other. Let me include staff and friends who I have had the pleasure of working with during this pandemic and during the process of writing this book: Ted, Kelly, Nikki, Aubree, Amber and Gabri Ella. These people have taught me so much about giving of myself, and I hope they have learned from me as well.

MCH Family Outreach is an awesome ministry that helps families, and my role as a case manager puts me in position to influence the clients that I serve daily. I want to influence the families that I come in contact with to become greater!

Life lesson from this chapter:

I was made to impact and influence others around me. I am responsible for the people of my own house. I am required to influence them first!

Take Care of Yourself!

I cannot recall the number of times that I have shared with others this advice: take care of yourself. Many times I have said to others, "Take time out for yourself." I have heard that we teach others what we need to learn for ourselves. Self-care is so vital to becoming greater. It's necessary to our mental well-being as it is to our physical health. This is something that I struggle with. Like most people, I want and wish for more hours in the day. If it were only that easy, and if I did have more hours in the day, would that be enough time in the day? Time is the only thing that we can never get back. That is why spending time taking care of ourselves is so important. It has taken me almost a lifetime to find or make time to just relax.

I have the love of music. I listen to music every day, I mean, literally every day. There are a few days when I do not get to listen to music, and I feel empty and lost. Music has been my way to escape, to lose myself after a long day. That is what a person needs to do: find ways to lose themselves, do things that bring them joy and relaxation. For me, its music. What is it for you? Self-care is all about losing yourself and at the same time finding yourself too. The road to self-care leads us to the path of finding out about ourselves.

When I listen to music, I find that this opens my mind up writing more. I get more ideas on things that I want to write about. My mind is free to explore new things that interest me, new things like paint by number. This is my latest self-care hobby. A fellow coworker got me interested in this paint by number. I love the time that I spend painting and just thinking about what I will write about next. I am realizing that when I paint, it is very relaxing, and it takes my mind away from whatever is going on around me. I am learning more and

95

more the importance of taking time for myself. I am learning to love myself as well. The more I love myself I find that I do not have to feel guilty about placing me first!

Look within and discover who you are. Honor this person every moment of each day.

Learn to invest in yourself. It will be the greatest payoff ever. This is the time in your life when you go out on faith and become greater. Throughout this book, you have learned how you made for greatness. Here is when you begin to make good on that. Self-care is about that, taking care of yourself, putting yourself first for a change, learning that new hobby. Everyone's self-care looks different. What does your self-care look like? Your self-care will not look like mine, but we both need it whatever it looks like. We both have days that are filled with more questions than answers. This will leave us over-whelmed and confused. Always keep in mind that there is only so many hours in the day. You work eight, play eight, and sleep eight! It was explained to me like this years ago, even though it never works out like this. We all have the same time each day, twenty-four hours. If you learn nothing else from this book, make note of this: you cannot do everything in one day! You cannot change the world all by yourself in one day! I have seen and known many people who have suffered burnout because of trying to do more than they could ever do without taking care of themselves first. Earlier in this book, I wrote about learning to say *no*. I have learned over a course of time that saying no is vital to self-care. This is important in learning to take care of ourselves. I have also struggled with this, saying no when so many times I knew that I was putting myself in a position that I would regret later. In my opinion, self-care is all about knowing your limits, knowing when to say no, and walking away from situations that will put us in difficult situations. Plain and simple, if it doesn't feel good or feel right, don't do it! Always follow your gut feeling. It never lies! My gut has never lied to me, never. Looking back over my life, to this very day, had I followed my gut instincts, I could have saved myself from much pain and turmoil. Self-care is about listening to yourself and following those instincts.

Loving yourself is a huge part of self-care. Loving who you are, being okay with who you are. Once I had a friend ask me during a phone conversation if I love myself. The question caught me off guard at first, but after thinking about it, it really made me think. *Do I really love myself?* I am a people pleaser. I have spent the biggest part of my adult life doing for others, seeking the love and affirmation from others. People pleasers put others first. This is who I am. I have been this way for a long time. Even as a child, I wanted to be a people pleaser, always putting others before myself. People pleasers are the worst at self-care. They neglect taking care of themselves and taking time for themselves. Life lesson here.

Reset.
Restart.
Refocus.
As many times as you need to.

I have very few days when I do absolutely nothing! Those days are far in between, not enough of them. But I do enjoy days that I simply take time for myself, time to relax and listen to my music or start a new paint by number. Self-care is also about distancing yourself from negativity and the people who drain the life out of you, you know, the ones who are depressing to be around. They see all the wrong, nothing pleases them. They tell you that you are wasting your time when you want to do something positive. They always have an opinion about everything but never any solutions! You know the type. You and I both know the type here. These are people you want to stay clear from. This is a part of self-care. I have literally been around this type of person and think, *Why are they even in my circle?* They leave you drained, and you need to recharge your own self. Not everyone is good to be around with, as my daddy would often say. Not everyone is on the level you are currently on. When that happens, you can find yourself trying to level up back to where you once were at. This will drain you both emotionally and mentally. To avoid this, you must practice self-care. Take care of yourself—mind, body, and soul—always.

It has taken me a long time to learn the importance of taking time for me, the importance of getting proper rest and sleep, time to just sit and do nothing. My dad instilled in me as a young child that if you sit and do nothing, you are lazy! All my life I thought that sitting idle meant that I was lazy, and I never wanted to come across as lazy, so I worked my tail off. I have been this way for years, but I see now that I must refresh and refocus, and that takes self-care. It has nothing to do with being lazy. We all need this in our lives. I recently had a conversation with a coworker about our roles at work as case managers. We work daily with other people's problems, helping them through difficult times, then we go home sometimes mentally and emotionally exhausted. This requires self-care on our part, time to unwind and refresh for the next day. Some days cannot end soon enough depending on the client case load, but when it does, you need that time to focus on yourself.

The social work field has taught me this one thing. While we work with hurting people, most of the time it takes a heart of compassion and empathy to do this type of work. You love what you do for a living. You love helping hurting people. But, most of all, find love for yourself. I touched on this earlier in this chapter about loving yourself. Find the time to love yourself in the process of loving and helping others. You are just as important, if not even more important. If you don't take care of yourself, you will not be able to help others. We hear this a lot in this field of work. Self-care is vital in any field of work today. The occupation does not matter, high-stress job or not. Stress will find a way to find you! Be ready when it does. Know how you will react to it. Know what it takes to take care of yourself. Know your limits and boundaries. Set limits and boundaries if you need to in order to practice self-care. This is so important to your well-being. I have learned this in my lifetime about givers. People who give and give of themselves, they always are first in line to help, to see what they can do to make the situation better. They show up first to help and are last to leave. Takers, on the other hand, fly by different rules. They usually don't have any! They will drain you until you are empty.

Take care of yourself! My goal for the coming new year is to take more time out for myself. This is an area of my life that must improve. I want to have days that I have less to do and more time to do things that I enjoy doing. I will let you know how this all plays out!

Givers have to learn to set limits because takers don't have any.

Ask yourself, what will I do to better take care of my well-being? What am I willing to do that will ensure that I spend time doing something that brings my joy? For self-care to take place, you must be willing to change. You must be open for change, change such as accepting the fact that you deserve peace of mind, you deserve to be happy. You are responsible for your own happiness. It's not your job or spouse, your career or education that will bring you happiness. It all depends on you and your attitude toward life and those things around you. Yes, you create your own happiness! If you learn nothing else from this chapter, remember this: do not let anyone take away your happiness. Never allow that to happen, another reason why self-care is so important. I am at the point of my life where my self-care and well-being must be at the front of all that I do these days. I need to make more time for myself to enjoy the things that bring me joy and happiness. You should want the same for yourself. You should want to bring your own happiness to your world. This, my friend, is your power! No one can nor should be able to control this but you. Your happiness is important to your well-being when it comes to self-care. When you master this in your life, you will be on your way to becoming better at being you!

Self-care may also look like deleting certain people out of your life. Not everyone was meant to do life with you for life. Some people will not be with you until the end. This is also part of taking care of yourself. Delete or unfriend accordingly as you see fit. I mentioned this earlier about loving yourself: find out what that looks like and what will it take to love yourself. This process will help in self-care for yourself and becoming the person you were meant to be. It will help in finding the greatness that is within you. I cannot stress enough when I mention about loving yourself. People that pour out from themselves usually leave the tank empty when it comes to themselves. Helping someone else and neglecting yourself is not beneficial to anyone involved here. Always remember yourself, always! I truly believe in taking time for yourself. This is an area that I struggle with myself. I want to work in this area of my life more and more, taking time to relax and spending more time enjoying myself. This is a vital life lesson, learning to relax. Some people have no problem with this. Many have already mastered this concept. But there are many who have yet to grasp the concept of self-care and the importance of spending time relaxing.

If you don't pick a day to relax, your body will pick it for you.

I can recall that as I was growing up, my father did not do much on Sundays! This was his time to relax and unwind. Although there were times that he did have to work, but rest was on the agenda on Sundays. I am learning this as I grow older: the importance of relaxing, how I need to take it easy more. As much as I love to give of my time volunteering, I also know there are times when I choose to just relax and to stay home with no guilt. Give yourself the time to grow and flourish. Give yourself room for improvement, to make choices that will help you expand your horizons in life. I have known people who worked all their lives and finally retire after forty plus years of service, then suddenly come down with poor health and die! Having never enjoyed the retirement years, the traveling and sightseeing. Time is so precious. Time is the only thing we can never get back. Each moment we live is gone. Tomorrow will never play itself back again. Two minutes ago will never come around again; it's simply gone. Take care of the time you have and use it wisely. Learn to be good to yourself. It's not selfish; it's necessary. I was talking to a friend the other day and stated that this is an area of my life that I need to improve on, time set aside for me. Maybe you need to do the same. I find that as I grow older, time to rest and do nothing is so vital to my overall health. Learn this concept as well. Learn to take care of yourself. Spend time doing what makes you happy, and spend lots of time doing just that.

**One day you will look back and realize
that you worried too much
about things that really don't matter.**

Life lesson from this chapter:

If you don't take care of yourself, no one else will! You are responsible for your own happiness!

Note to Self

I know you are doing the best you can. I can see that there have been struggles in your life. Keep pressing forward, keep moving, and keep climbing. You have accomplished much when many counted you out. I have been both laughed at and praised, sometimes by the same people! There have been times when the people who were close to me hurt me the most, both family and friends, but isn't it always this way? You have never been hurt by an enemy, if you think about it. The hurt always has come from those who love you. But even then, you made it through. You just moved on. Lesson learned. You have learned both to love and let go! Life has not always been fair to you, but here you are, the scars and bruises that you have endured to be here.

You grew up with humble beginnings in life, modest to say the least, no running water indoor, no central air or heat; but here you are. The house was cold in the winter and hot in the summer, windows with no screens. You have made it to this point because you have fought through the struggles in life. You have gone without, and you have made things happen with what you had to work with. Life is full of twist and turns. So much happens in the course of time, good and the bad. You have been on both sides. You have had plenty, and you have been in want. You know what it is like to not have enough. Boy, do you know what this is like! This too has been a life lesson, probably your greatest lesson of all. Growing up poor made you tougher than the average kid. It made you more aware of what is important in life, the basics. You survived with what you were given, and that was not very much in terms of material things. Recall years ago when you were out of work for almost two years, getting a job in a field of work that was new to you, recall asking your cousin, "Can we do this type of work?" His response was "Yes, we can. We are survivors." He also said, "Look at where we came from." We will survive! He was right. Years have passed, and you are still surviving. You can do this; you were made for this.

That time when you were without a job for almost two years! You were made for that. You grew during that time. You never once went without eating, not one bill not paid. You survived yet again. Please learn to forgive yourself. This is something you have struggled with all your adulthood life. Learn to forgive yourself and move on. Learn to let go of your past mistakes. This will be a life lesson you can learn much from. Learn to give your own self grace. You have forgiven others all your life. Some did not even deserve it, but you took the high road and let them make it. Do the same for yourself! Let yourself make it; you deserve it! Remember those times when people walked over you, talked about you, lied on you? Not once did you hold hatred in your heart for them. You always have said that you treated them better than they treated you. Yes, give yourself the same grace. Love yourself with all you have. Keep dreaming. Never stop dreaming. Never stop thinking big! When you were a little kid, you dreamed big. You dreamed about doing great things, helping others to live a better life. You saw this at an early age. Keep dreaming. You are in the position that you have dreamed to be in: helping others who are in need, being in position to make a difference. You were made for this.

God's plan is bigger than your mistakes.

Never stop loving those around you. Love has gotten you this far in life. You have loved the unlovable. Those who have hurt you the most have gotten the most love in return from you. Love was a lesson taught to you years ago. A loving and caring mother was the perfect example of love. You saw love each day because of her love for you and others. You have made it known that your mother and father were your greatest influences in your life. You would never be the person you are if not for them. Whatever you do in life, keep them near to your heart. Make moves that would make them both feel proud of you. Always make them proud of you, and know that you will see them again one day in heaven.

That time when you quit that job that you loved so much doing, but because of poor leadership and a toxic work environment you left, you returned after being gone a few months. This was a hard decision to make, but you made the best of it. Never had you ever quit a job to go back to the same job, but you knew your work ethic would open the door for you again. A man's gift will make room for him. You have believed this for some time, and it is true. You learned a valuable lesson through this experience. You learned the importance of having a good name. You learned that your name and work ethic will follow you no matter where you go in life. This is something that your dad taught you long ago.

You have learned to forgive and forget and move on. This is the biggest life lesson you have learned in this past year. People come into your life to teach you a lesson. They come in for a season or a reason! Some come to stay with you, and others are not meant to stay. They are meant to move on. Their part in your life is over. It happens. Don't fret over this. Move on. Sometimes no explanation is even needed. You have learned also that life is summed up in three words: "It goes on." Hold your head up. Life has not always been so good to you, but God has! Life can be so cruel. It's been not fair at times, but here you are. A survivor is what your cousin called you years ago, that day when you were in the car with him going to new employee orientation at a mental health (mental retardation) facility. You applied for a job you knew nothing about, but you knew you had a family to care for and you had responsibilities to take care off. Your cousin said to you, "We are survivors. We come from the bottom with nothing." We have lived to see the hardest of days. Here you are! Life will continue to teach you what you need to know. The best school and class is life itself. Keep learning from it. You have done the best with life has given you. You have learned from the good and the bad. You have fought to be where you are now. The success has not come easy, and you still press forward. You persist with all that you have within you. The cotton fields made you stronger. Even the tireless hours in the hot sun taught you a lesson. The hot summer heat taught you that you wanted to always do better in life. You wanted to make something of yourself. You wanted to make your mom and dad proud of you. Believe in your heart always that you accomplished this goal in life, that they would be so proud of you today. God knows you have done so many things that they would not approve of. Maybe this time you finally got it right, like that day you graduated from college, how you sat there waiting for your name to be called out to walk the stage. You thought of your mother, how you wished she was there to see you on your big day.

One thing that you have learned this year during the pandemic is that it is time to fix things that you have made wrong. Fix some friendships and some you had to say goodbye to just to get your mind on the right track. Goodbyes are sometimes necessary. They are needed for our mental state of being. You did what needed to be done. You are still a work in progress. You still are learning to speak up for yourself. Whatever you do, keep trusting God. He promises to never leave you, nor forsake you. You have left him many times over and over, but he has never left you once. God will always know your heart. He will never hold anything against you. Even in all your sinful ways, he remains faithful, and he loves you unconditionally. The love that God has for you is beyond any love you will ever experience in this life. He simply cannot ever not love you! Stay with God; he will stay with you is something you have always heard. But I am here to say that he will stay with you no matter what. Learn to love yourself more each day. You deserve it!

Never stop believing in yourself. Always trust your gut; it has never lied to you. Dream like never before, and dream big! You are a product from poverty. No one really expected you to do well in life. Even you didn't believe that you would. Never doubt yourself. Always know that you have achieved more than expected. You got this. This has always been your struggle. This has always been your vice, believing in yourself. This has cost you so much—lack of confidence, lack of self-esteem—but here you are. You have grown to be a confident person with so much to offer this world in terms of helping the helpless and hopeless. You are doing the best that you can. You are making things happen that brings change to others daily. You have days when you feel you are not doing enough, but you follow through anyways. You are persistent. Keep doing what you are doing. I know that not everyone cheers you on. Not everyone claps when you win, but you remain steadfast and hopeful knowing all that matters is that you believe in yourself. Always keep your circle small with the ones who will stand with you until the end. You know the ones. Not everyone who started out with you are still with you. Their place in your life is over for whatever reason, but you are still standing. You have survived so many trials and tribulations by the grace of God. The hot cotton fields could not hurt you; the cold winters in a house with no running water or decent heat could not hurt you. You have experienced both plenty and want. You are still standing! Never stop being who you were created to be. You were made for greatness! Never stop short of being the person you were made to be in this cruel world. Many times, when you should have given people a piece of your mind, you gave them your heart instead. This hurt you more, but you provided them help and hope something this cruel world needs so badly. Keep being great in the presence of others. Keep loving, forgiving, helping, caring, giving. These are all traits of greatness. You were made for this moment. Right now is your time to shine! You have learned throughout this life that nothing stays the same. Things change in the twinkling of an eye. The rain comes, and the sun shines the next day. Troubles come and go. Even our trials do not stay with us forever. Keep being grateful for the blessings in your life. You have so much to say thank you for. Looking back at your life, from that small wood-framed house with the dirt road at the front of the yard, be thankful.

Forgive your younger self.
Believe in your current self.
Create your future self.

You are blessed beyond measure; you tell yourself this often. Keep blessing those around you as much as possible. Keep giving when you can. This will open the doors to many more blessings in your life. It all starts with how you give and how often you give. You have often said that if you won the lottery, you would just give it all away! Keep that attitude with you always: to put others before yourself. This can be both a blessing and a curse in your life, but at the end of the day, bless others often. Keep being kind as often to this cruel world. This display of kindness was taught to you by your parents. You had great examples by your mom and dad. Never forget the talks your daddy had with you while riding to the pasture to feed the cows. Daddy talked to you like you were a grown man. You were just a young boy, but he was always preparing you for this mean world with advice, like be careful who you become friends with and it's okay to be a loner.

Every day is a new day to learn something. What did you learn today? What does a ten- or twelve-year boy learn about life daily? Daddy always wanted an answer, and he taught me to always give an answer. Having a conversation with a reader of you book, *The Silent Dreamer*, recently. You were told that this is your time! You were made for this moment. It's your time to shine! You have waited your entire life to be where you are right now. Flourish and be the person God intended for you to be. Everyone makes mistakes. You have had your share of them. Keep going. Stay on the course. Your best days are in front of you! This is the year where you wanted increase. You wanted growth. You wanted successes and wins! You will get all that you have asked for and more if you trust the process and trust his timing! You were made to be greater, kinder, thankful! You have a made-up mind! Your gift will make plenty of room for you. You are next-level ready! Your future is not your past! Keep learning to say *no*! This is the key to your self-care! This is your time. Why not now, and why not you? You have no room for bitterness in your life. Move on and value the lesson. *The Silent Dreamer* was just the beginning. You have so much more to say, so many stories to tell. The roll call of influencers that were mentioned are rooting for you. Those who have passed on are smiling down at you. They are still a huge part of your life and always will be. You may have lost all your mentors, mother and father figures from years past, but you have wonderful memories. They watch you from above. I am at the point of closing this book.

This chapter was written for anyone that may be at the crossroads of life, the person who feels like they have not yet reached full potential in their life. Keep moving forward. You are doing well. Keep going. Someone needs to forgive themselves who is reading this now. Forgive yourself! It's your time to let go and grow! Someone is undecided about their career, the job they are on. It's time for change. Today is your day to start something new! This part was written just for you. Someone is struggling with giving so much of themselves and not getting the same in return. This was written just for you. Your time is coming. Hold on to the love you give. It's your time to receive it back in full. Your time to be great is *now*! This is your time to shine! Trust the process, the timing. It's your time for *Pathway to Greatness*! *Never stop dreaming!*

Note to self:

When things feel overwhelming, remember:
One thought at a time.
One task at a time.
One day at a time.

Life lesson from this chapter:

Take life one day at a time. Forgive yourself as you forgive others!

Follow me on social media:
Johnny Martinez-Carroll, author on Facebook
@dreambig_johnny on Twitter
www.johnnymartinezcarroll.com

About the Author

Johnny Martinez-Carroll lives in rural Central Texas, in the small community of Snook. Johnny received his education from the University of Phoenix, bachelor's degree in human service management, class of 2016. Johnny Martinez-Carroll works for a local nonprofit, Methodist Children's Home, as a case manager. Johnny Martinez-Carroll published his first book, *The Silent Dreamer*, in 2020. His book was selected to be featured at the Texas Word Wranglers Book Festival 2021. This is a prestigious book festival held in Giddings Texas, Martinez-Carroll was a featured author for his work on *The Silent Dreamer*. Johnny Martinez-Carroll is also a certified life coach and loves to encourage and inspire young minds. Johnny Martinez-Carroll and his wife, Sue, have adult kids and spend their time with grandkids. In his spare time, Martinez-Carroll loves to give back to his community by volunteering and making himself available to the needs of the less fortunate, whether its volunteering with Habitat for Humanity or building beds for a local nonprofit, Sleep in Heavenly Peace. Martinez-Carroll believes we are here to make the world a better place. To learn more about Johnny Martinez-Carroll, visit his website: www.johnnymartinezcarroll.com.

CPSIA information can be obtained
at www.ICGtesting.com
Printed in the USA
JSHW050026201122
33507JS00001B/55

9 798885 404839